Women in Computing

G L Simons

PUBLISHED BY NCC PUBLICATIONS

British Library Cataloguing in Publication Data

Simons, G. L.
  Women in computing.
  1. Computer industry – Great Britain – Employees
  2. Women – Employment – Great Britain
  I. Title
  338.4'7'001640941   HD 9696.C62
  ISBN 0-85012-296-1

To Chris (successful in a man's world), Corinne and Colette (who
will be) and Conrad and Cornel (who will expect nothing less).
                                                    Geoff Simons

First published in 1981 by:

NCC Publications, The National Computing Centre Limited,
Oxford Road, Manchester M1 7ED, England.

Printed in England by UPS Blackburn Limited

Typeset in 11pt Press Roman by Focal Design Studios Limited,
New Mills, Stockport, Cheshire.

ISBN 0-85012-296-1

Acknowledgments

Various companies, other organisations and individuals were approached for information. Some individuals showed great interest in the project and I am grateful to them for their support and suggestions. Particular thanks are due to:

Pamela Poe (Key Communications Ltd) for contributing the excellent case studies (Appendix 1) of Dataskil staff, and for her comments.

Thanks are also due to the following for variously providing photographs, brochures, photocopies of articles, and other material:

F International Ltd (I am particularly grateful to Mrs Steve Shirley for making her own files freely available and to Mrs Rosemary Symons for her support)

Pamela Woodman (Pamela Woodman Associates)

Pamela Morton (Thames Polytechnic)

Robert Sherry (Robert Sherry & Associates)

Equal Opportunities Commission (EOC)

Institute of Personnel Management

Manchester Business School

Members of the Women in Computing Group, A Woman's Place, for discussing attitudes and trends.

NCC staff have helped in various ways. I would thank Godfrey Hall for his comments, and thanks are also due to Christine Marshall for helping with research, translation and other tasks; to Janice Wooding for being alert to relevant material appearing in the journals and to Edna Taylor for typing to her usual high standard the whole of the first draft.

G L Simons
Chief Editor, NCC Publications

Introduction

There is growing awareness of the rights of women in society, a growing consciousness that it is indefensible to discriminate — in employment and other areas — on the basis of a person's sex. The heightened awareness has yielded new legislation in many countries, new attitudes in companies, and increased self-confidence on the part of women.

No particular industry is immune from the attitudes of the broader culture. Discriminatory assumptions in society as a whole will be reflected, to a greater or lesser extent, in particular sectors of industrial activity. The data processing industry is no exception, though many observers suggest that in this relatively new sector there is less prejudice against women than in older, more traditional industries.

The extent to which anti-women discrimination exists in the data processing industry is influenced by such factors as the shortage of skilled labour, the impact of economic and commercial circumstances, and the pressure of attitudes in the broader culture. It is important to realise that the international data processing industry has many sectors: ranging from sweatshop manufacture of silicon chips in the Third World to up-market consultancy in the developed countries. When we talk of 'women in computing' we tend to think of operators or programmers, rarely of Asian women toiling long (and often unhealthy) hours fabricating electronic components. But the sector concerned with primary manufacture is very important: in an obvious sense it supports the more comfortable spectrum of data processing jobs in the advanced nations.

To some extent the position of women in the data processing

industry is here considered against the broader employment and legislative considerations. Women's progress in computing cannot proceed in isolation from progress in general employment attitudes, law, education and other fields. A brief profile is included of the concept of stereotyping, and mention is made of traditional assumptions as to why women may make unsatisfactory employees − assumptions that, in the literature, are increasingly being dubbed 'myths'. There are also brief profiles of successful women in data processing. (The second part of Appendix 3 lists the women, and men, who are mentioned in text − though in no sense should this list be interpreted as a Who's Who of dp women. The list is intended to be illustrative, not exhaustive.)

There are some suggestions as to steps that should be taken to improve the position of women in computing, though any *full* treatment is outside the scope of the present book. It is encouraging that a women's group* has recently been formed to act constructively in this area (interested people should contact Women and Computing, c/o A Woman's Place, 48 William IV Street, London WC2). This group parallels similar organisations in the US (see Chapter 1).

Women are making progress in computing, as they are in other employment fields, but it is important for people not to be complacent about any gains in the present situation. Women are still mostly employed in low-grade dp work, representing only a tiny proportion of managerial staff in companies and other organisations. And there are some suggestions that the relative position of women in employment has even worsened in recent years, partly as a result of general economic trends.

There is no doubt, taking a long-term perspective, that women are making social progress. We have all managed to emancipate ourselves from some of the more bizarre historical attitudes. In the sixth century, the bishops attending a synod in Macon (Gaul) debated earnestly whether women were human beings; Thomas Aquinas later defined woman as a 'failed man' (*mas occasionatus*); in the sixteenth century, women were regarded as mid-way between apes and men; and in the nineteenth, Charles Darwin claimed that

* See Liz Else, Women's Group Marks Trend, *Computing*, 12/2/81. p 10; and Data for the Girls, *The Guardian*, 23/2/81.

man attained to a higher eminence, 'in whatever he takes up, than can woman — whether requiring deep thought, reason, or imagination, or merely the use of the senses and hands.' Today we are largely free of such distorted attitudes, but many current assumptions may come to seem as almost equally irrational as the myths and falsehoods of the past.

One aim of the present book is to stimulate discussion, perhaps to open up new lines of enquiry, and to encourage a search for constructive policies on the part of managers, employers, politicians and others. Apart from the simple claims of justice, there is a certain economic perversity in neglecting the human resources that reside in half the population of the world. The computer industry is proud of its modern, progressive image. Many observers believe that in its treatment of women there is room for improvement.

Contents

	Page
Acknowledgments	5
Introduction	7
1 Background	**15**
Introduction	15
Employment	15
General	15
Pay	16
Job Security	18
The Data Processing Industry	18
Women in Data Processing	26
Media Attitudes	32
Summary	37
2 Equality or Discrimination?	**41**
Introduction	41
Stereotyping	42
Legislation	43
Employment in General	45
Data Processing Industry	54
General	54
Particular Occupations	55
The Manufacturing Base	56
Discriminatory Trends and Patterns	59
Summary	71

Education 72
Summary 80

3 Women in Management 83

Introduction 83
Discrimination 85
Attitudes to Female Managers 88
Current Plans to Advance Women 90
Female Characteristics, Stress 93
Profiles of Female Managers 100
Steps to Take 104
Summary 107

4 The Office Environment 109

Introduction 109
Discrimination 111
The Impact of Office Automation 112
   Employment 112
   Job Deskilling 118
   Health 123
Summary 128

5 Freelance and Home-Based Work 131

Introduction 131
Home-Based Work 132
F International Group 136
Heights Inc 141
Pamela Woodman Associates 142
Robert Sherry & Associates 144
ICL Contract Programming 145
Summary 146

6 The Future 149

Introduction 149
Conditions for Change 150
Steps to Take 150
Summary 151

Appendices

1 Case Studies 153

2 Bibliography 167

3 Plates 181

4 Index 195
    Subjects 197
    Names 207

1   Background

INTRODUCTION

The position of women in computing — like any other social circumstance — is conditioned by many factors. It is obvious that the innate or acquired psychological and intellectual qualities of people are highly relevant. So too are the male and female *perceptions* of such qualities. If female talent is perceived, by both men and women, in prejudiced terms there will be inevitable constraints on the advancement of women in society.

There is some evidence in the computer industry of prejudice against women (some evidence is provided in the present chapter, some in Chapters 2 and 3). Part of the problem is that much of this prejudice is shared by women — an inevitable consequence of the cultural pressures. This circumstance is bound to influence a woman's self-image, her self-confidence, and her social and career expectations.

In the present chapter we consider employment in general terms and provide some information about the data processing industry. Following a brief profile of some significant contributions made to computing by women, we indicate ways in which particular female images are still conveyed in computer literature.

EMPLOYMENT

General

It is a common complaint of women seeking employment or career development that employers, usually male, are excessively influenced by media images, by 'stereotyping', and by other 'sexist' preconceptions. This type of complaint needs to be evaluated with care. There is an obvious temptation in some circumstances for a person to adopt a *scapegoating* interpretation of events: a woman may wrongly attribute her failure in a job interview to male prejudice. She may not subsequently learn that the *successful* applicant was a woman, and may simply use her own failure as bogus evidence for social injustice.

However, while the possibility of scapegoating needs to be mentioned it cannot explain the bulk of female resentment — where it exists — in the employment situation. Many people would argue that there is still widespread prejudice against women as employees, and that this is seen in discriminatory attitudes that affect women's pay, job definitions, employment security, and opportunities for advancement. It is a fact that women on average earn less than men. They do not receive the same training opportunities in many organisations, and they are less likely to achieve management or professional jobs.

Pay

Though women now constitute more than 40% of the UK workforce, they earn considerably less than men, even allowing for the fact they they work shorter hours and do less overtime. The Equal Pay Act, which came into effect at the end of 1975, had an impact on women's pay but much less than many people hoped. And the rate of progress towards equality has in fact declined since 1976. By April 1978 there was evidence that the gap was beginning to widen. Consider Table 1 (source: *Department of Employment Gazette*).

It is also significant that women are very unevenly distributed throughout the workforce, tending to appear predominantly in a range of low-paid jobs. Again there is evidence that this situation is getting worse. In 1966, just three service industries accommodated 52% of working women, but by 1978 the figure had risen to 58%, distributed as follows:

- 27% in professional and scientific services (typists, secretaries, technicians, teachers and nurses);

- 16% in distributive trades (shops, mail order, warehouses);

All Occupations	Males (pence/hour)	Females (pence/hour)	Females as % of Males
1972	83.3	53.9	64.7
1974	107.2	70.6	65.9
1975	139.3	98.3	70.6
1977	181.5	133.9	73.8
1978	204.9	148.0	72.2
1979	232.4	165.7	71.3
Manual Occupations			
1972	69.1	42.6	61.6
1974	91.1	58.7	64.4
1975	119.2	81.1	68.0
1977	154.3	110.7	71.7
1978	172.8	124.4	72.0
1979	197.5	138.7	70.2
Non-manual Occupations			
1972	110.8	59.8	54.0
1974	138.1	76.7	55.5
1975	174.6	105.9	60.7
1977	227.9	143.7	63.1
1978	257.9	157.9	61.2
1979	289.5	176.6	61.0

Table 1 Average Hourly Earnings of Full-time Adult Males and Females

— 15% in miscellaneous services (laundries, catering, dry clean-
ing, hairdressing).

In September 1980 a Low Pay Unit research project funded by
the Equal Opportunities Commission published a report, *Minimum
Wages for Women*. In October Mr Chris Pond, director of the unit,
declared that nearly 11,000 companies were underpaying workers
(mainly women), cheating them out of £22 million a year. He
suggested that more than two million women workers are underpaid.

Where women enter low-pay occupations, where they significantly outnumber men (eg 91% of typists, secretaries and short-
hand writers are female, 76% of workers in clothing and footwear
manufacture), it is difficult to invoke the provisions of the Equal
Pay Act. For the Act to be effective in an individual claim a
woman needs to be able to compare her work with that of a man.

Job Security

In circumstances of economic recession and new technology there
tends to be less job security for women than for men. Many industries that have traditionally employed large numbers of women
(eg clothing, footwear and textiles) are declining in the UK, and
with cuts in public spending, opportunities in teaching are declining. New technology is affecting women's employment in the service industries, and in clerical work, and in other areas.

The traditional role of women in light industry, including the
manufacture of printed circuit boards for computers, has scarcely
changed over recent years. In most UK electronics factories, the
great majority of the unskilled workers are women, and their jobs
are under threat. It is now possible to automate such jobs as insert-
ing components into printed-circuit boards, soldering connections,
circuit testing, and packing. It is less easy to automate the more
highly-skilled jobs, but in these occupations there is a lower proportion of women.

The Data Processing Industry

Data processing, as a new industry, should be less subject to traditional prejudice and the resulting discriminatory practices. In fact

discrimination against women can be discerned here as elsewhere (see Chapters 2 and 3), though there is debate as to its extent. To some degree a demeaning or patronising view of women is conveyed in technical computing journals and books, reflecting attitudes of the broader culture. And the lower the grade in a computing organisation the higher the proportion of women tends to be: for example, there is a relatively high proportion of female keypunch operators but female data processing managers are rare (see Chapter 3).

In the UK manufacture of electronic computers in 1980, there were about 36,000 men and about 13,000 women employed, with a relatively large proportion of the women engaged in lowly assembly and testing tasks. The pattern here is much as it is in other manufacturing industries. It seems to be assumed that women can be employed at low cost in low-grade work, and that the higher the employment grade in the organisational hierarchy the smaller the proportion of women. A different pattern is encountered in bureaux, software houses and other non-manufacturing companies, though it is generally assumed that typists, receptionists and switchboard operators will be women.

A recent (1980) International Congress for Data Processing, held in West Berlin, covered as main humanitarian themes the influence of computers on work, privacy, Third World countries, and the position of women in the data processing industry. In an opening address Eckhard Fuchs, the conference chairman, appealed for these emotive subjects to be discussed frankly between dp experts, trade unionists and employers ('Those engaged in data processing are at present the only ones able to identify and describe such topics'). It was pointed out that in the data processing industry women were still frequently confined to data entry and keyboarding jobs. In this respect the women who addressed the conference were atypical: they had all advanced a considerable way along their respective paths within the industry.

A significant proportion of the international female speakers suggested that, unless there is a significant change of attitudes within data processing, as the industry ascends in importance in society women can expect to be less and less a part of it. Initially it appeared that women had the same opportunities as men in data processing: it was a new profession and needed skills that had yet to be developed. But now, as 'on the job' training becomes more important to keep up with developments, there are signs that women are being left behind.

Kirsti Berg, a Norwegian consultant, argued that the position of women in data processing was not radically different to their position in society ('The position today for women in data processing is not different from their position in society in general. From the point of view of equal rights we can expect this to get worse'). Other speakers agreed with this analysis, presenting statistics for their own countries, including the UK, the US and West Germany (see Chapter 2). In all the countries where relevant statistics were available it was found that

— women work most frequently in the lower-paid grades in the computer industry;

— women are often paid less than men in the same grades, despite equal-pay legislation.

In circumstances of rapid technological change the vital nature of suitable training and education is emphasised. Again there is evidence that women are losing out. Thus, Christine Fürstin von Urach, a senior officer project director in Daimler-Benz of Stuttgart declared: 'Women are now giving up an area that they have already conquered because they are not getting the training that they need.' And fears were even expressed that if the shortage in data processing staff ever ends then women will find themselves being demoted into the ranks of keypunch and keyboard operators.

Even where there is a pressing need for more data processing specialists there often seems to be reluctance on the part of managements — usually predominantly male — to recruit and train suitable women. This point is emphasised in a recent ASTMS booklet, *Computer Professionals* — 'There is little incentive or encouragement from the industry to recruit and train female graduates with suitable aptitude who may have been channelled by the higher education system into obtaining arts degrees rather than the traditional male-oriented engineering and science qualifications.' And an example is given from the related area of telecommunications: in this field, official 1978 Department of Employment statistics showed that only 1.06% of all professionally qualified staff were women. At the same time, a NEDO Computer Sector Working Party report, in common with other surveys, highlighted specialist staff shortages.

The response of women to discrimination in employment is part of a heightened female consciousness in modern society. Women's groups have sprung up in many countries to discuss the circumstances of discrimination, domestic issues, and how women can advance to equality. A number of these groups, particularly in the US, focus on science and technology.

The American *Association for Women in Science* (AWIS) was formed in 1971 as a national organisation 'to promote equal opportunities for women to enter the professions and to achieve their career goals.' The organisation affirms that women have the intrinsic ability to function as competently as men in science, and recognises the necessity to take a firm public stand on matters of discrimination which affect the careers of women.

The AWIS registry contains biographies of more than 5000 women scientists, and serves as an employment clearing house for government, industry and the academic world. The Association monitors agencies of government mandated to protect women against sex discrimination, provides information to members of Congress and congressional committees, encourages solidarity amongst professional women, conducts meetings, provides career information, etc.

In 1974 the AWIS Educational Foundation was founded and incorporated to provide financial support for conferences and scholarships. The Foundation acted as a cosponsor with the New York Academy of Sciences in 1978 for a conference 'Expanding the Role of Women in the Sciences'. Membership of AWIS is open to both men and women.

The *Association for Women in Computing* (AWC) was formed in Washington, 5 December 1978, the aim being to 'promote communication among women in the data processing industry and to help further their professional development and advancement.' Anita Cochran, one of the organisers and a council member of the Association for Computing Machinery (ACM), observed that

'women know the rules but men know the ropes.' It is acknowledged that whereas the computer industry is generally considered
one of the better professions for women in the US, too many
women are confined to programming with too few in management.
A main AWC concern is that many dp women are employed in
data entry or types of programming that are likely to be overtaken
soon by technological advances.

It is also emphasised that women are held back because most
are not as well educated as men in the day-to-day aspect of a job,
because they do not communicate well with their male bosses or
colleagues, and because they are discouraged at school from studying mathematics and science. A central aim of AWC is to promote
the technical education of women of all ages and to encourage
women to follow technical career paths. Cochran has recognised
that there is much work to be done ('First we have to learn to
walk. Right now we're crawling, but soon we will be running').

In addition to AWC, there are the parallel US organisations,
Women in Data-Processing and *Women in Information Processing*.
Women in Data-Processing, based in New York, was founded 'on
the assumption that women have the power to shape their own
professional futures.' Again it is emphasised that special skills and
attitudes are required, that it is necessary for women to discard
the limitations imposed by childhood training, and that women
should strive to gain confidence and experience in competing in a
man's world.

Women in Information Processing (WIP), based in Washington,
is attempting to build up 'a feminine counterpart to the powerful
old boys' network' to advance the careers of the 300,000-plus
women in the US information processing community. The organisation is aiming to create a network of working women ('It helps
women help each other to win more clout, more pay, more know-
how and more self-esteem').

In the inaugural issue of WIP's publication, *Parity* (reported in
Computerworld, 22/9/80), Janice Miller, WIP president, spoke of
women's 'frustration from not understanding corporate gamesmanship and career development.' And she asks the question, 'What
good are brains, ambition and the taste of success if you don't
know what to do next to move ahead?' By the end of 1980, WIP

had evolved in one year into a national organisation claiming more than 500 members. Miller expects WIP to charter new chapters in other US cities.

The idea of 'networking', the establishment of 'old girl networks', is a common theme in many of the women's organisations. Thus AWC's Cochran has urged the use of a women's communication network to help women get into the right jobs. Male professionals have been accustomed to using such techniques by knowing 'the right man for the job.' Networking is seen as a means of breaking the 'old boy' networks, of helping women to develop their careers, and of building up female confidence by tackling their sense of alienation in employment. Like WIP's Miller, Cochran uses the word 'gamesmanship' to denote the techniques that women must learn to use in the employment situation.

Mary Scott Welch, author of *Networking* and a speaker at the recent (1980) networking session sponsored by Women in Data-Processing, has agreed that networking 'is not an extra'. On the contrary, 'it is every bit as important as being qualified or working hard — which women used to think was all that was important.' The networking session provided an opportunity for women to meet other women in data processing, to provide information, to increase contacts, and to find out the problems and activities of other women in data processing. Welch: 'Women should work 80% as hard and spend 20% of their time finding out what others are doing.'

Since women tend to be poorly represented in the higher echelons of a company they tend, as women, to be isolated. It has been emphasised that for a woman to ask a man for advice does not constitute an instance of networking. It is assumed, perhaps wrongly, that a man would not be sensitive to a woman's perspective, that for example, he would not understand a woman's concern at being the only woman at a meeting and being asked to take notes.

Women's groups have been formed in the US specifically for the purpose of networking. Such networks can embrace many industries (as with the efforts of the Association for Women in Science) or they can embrace one industry (as with AWC and WIP), or even a single company. Sometimes the internal networks will be sanc-

tioned by company management, recognising perhaps that effective exploitation of female talent is important to company success.
Networks may also relate specifically to a grade or profession.
Hence Welch has recently (late-1980) pointed out that special networks for female managers are being formed.

Networking, in a sense, implements the old trade union edict —
'organise'. It may be expected to gain momentum, to enable
women to identify discrimination, and to build up female solidarity and self-confidence.

There are many other types of advice being offered to women
who want to advance in data processing. For instance, Brenda
Pena, president of the New York chapter of the Association for
Women in Computing, is keen to get women into hardware. She
advises dp women to carry a screwdriver ('It's handy. You never
know when you're going to need it'). Pena has examined communications and technician jobs.

In communications there are seen to be real job opportunities,
but with the inevitable shortage of suitably trained women. Denise
Hassman, president of Women in Data-Processing, has indicated
the difficulty of getting female instructors for the telecommunications seminars. The problem facing women in communications has
been illustrated by two 1980 job advertisements in the *New York
Times*. In one, a 'fast-growing terminal supplier' was looking for
an electronics technician. The job required — 'one year technical
school training in digital and analogue circuitry with two to three
years' experience. Able to troubleshoot and repair to the component level on CRTs; impact, thermal and dot matrix printers; and
cassette tape drives.' Few women would have the technical training to apply for such a position.

The second advertisement was for telecommunications line
management professionals (job requirements: 'Experienced and
organised individuals to be responsible for installation and/or service repair groups. Will work as part of a highly professional and
closely integrated installation, implementation and maintenance
team. Need 5 to 10 years installation or field service. Supervisory
experience ... a well-organised decision maker, capable of working
under pressure'). Pena has pointed out that many women would
have the organisational, managerial and personnel skills for this

second job, but not the required technical skills (required by the second job and specified by the first).

Again it is emphasised — and this is equally true of the US, the UK, Europe and elsewhere — that at school women are less likely to be encouraged to opt for a technical career. They are encouraged instead to adopt secretarial or other service ambitions. Few women are encouraged to decide upon a career in electronics or electrical engineering, which again severely restricts the source of female entrants into communications engineering. (At the same time it has been suggested, by a man, that there is no shortage of women in communications. William J Leitman, an instructor in a telecommunications course, sees a situation of broad equality of opportunity — 'I see the computer industry as one in general where women have equal competitive advantage. Generally there's more acceptance of women.')

Some of the advice given to women is equally applicable to male workers in data processing. For example, Robert Brown, president of the Conec employment organisation (Framingham, Mass), speaking at the Greater Boston Chapter of the Association for Women in Computing, urged women in dp to know the market, to define their goals, to develop appropriate plans, and to continually monitor and adjust their career paths.

The address, as reported (*Computerworld*, 9/6/80), appears to make no allowance for particular problems faced by women. There is, however, acknowledgment of the value of networking — 'What we're establishing in meetings like this is a 'new girl network' as a counterpart to the 'old boy network.' It's astounding how fast information travels in such a network. You can find out about good companies, bad companies, good individuals and bad individuals; it's absolutely essential to people just starting out in the industry.'

There is increasing awareness that the problem of female advancement in data processing is multidimensional. It is impossible to separate attitudes to employment in computing (albeit a relatively new industry) from the broader and more traditional attitudes to employment in general. Nor can attitudes to employment be separated from attitudes to parental activity (eg the provision of child-care facilities), from attitudes of male spouses (eg will husbands really share chores?), and from education and training facilities prior to employment. The position of women in data processing can be tackled on a discrete and parochial basis, but there can be little doubt that where discrimination exists in the computing industry it reflects prejudices and inequalities that run through the broader community.

WOMEN IN DATA PROCESSING

Some women have contributed to female emancipation by scrutinising the institutional roots of discrimination. They have encouraged female 'consciousness raising', the creation of female solidarity in attitudes and employment, and an attack on traditional practices and assumptions. We have mentioned active women in the US — Miller, Hassman, Cochran, etc — who fall into this category and who work in data processing. Other women, less concerned with making overt political or ideological stands, have contributed to female emancipation by their own accomplishments in a male-dominated industry and in a male-dominated society.* Successful women in data processing, as in other fields, have helped to develop female confidence and self-esteem in what can be a hostile and demeaning environment.

It is often pointed out that the first programmer was a woman (see, for example, 'The Stormy Life of the World's First Programmer,' *Computer Weekly*, 10/1/80). Ada Lovelace, daughter of Lord Byron, was a gifted mathematician and carried out much of the programming work on Charles Babbage's Analytical Engine.

Lovelace met Babbage in 1833 at a party at which various scientific people were present. At that time Babbage was having difficulties over Treasury funding of development of his first calculating machine, the Difference Engine. In 1834 Lovelace attended lectures given by Dr Lardner on the machine.

When Babbage moved on to develop the ambitious Analytical Engine he seems to have provided no single coherent description of the machine or its programming (he was evidently poor on documentation!). The completeness of the best account we have is largely due to Lovelace.

* See also Profiles ... in Chapter 3 and Chapter 5.

Babbage had lectured in Turin, and a young Italian military engineer, L F Menabrea, wrote an account of the machine in French (published in October 1842). Lovelace translated the paper into English, whereupon Babbage encouraged her to write many detailed additions of her own. These additions included examples of programs which she had discussed with Babbage and which, with one exception, she had originated. She also discovered 'a grave mistake' in Babbage's suggestion for calculating Bernoulli numbers — perhaps the first recorded example of a program bug.

Lovelace expanded the Menabrea paper to three times its original length, delighting Babbage with this evident demonstration of the power of the Analytical Engine. She also demonstrated her own mathematical ability, apparently rebuking Babbage when he attempted to improve the style of her notes. In fact Babbage is reported as saying that Lovelace understood the Analytical Engine better than he did himself!

The introduction of index notation in the notes, to remove ambiguities, was Lovelace's initiative, as was discussion of the different sequences in which a set of operations could be carried out and the suggestion that correct choice of sequence would minimise the total time of calculation. She corrected some of the Menabrea formulae and tabulated the program operations to clarify the process. In her final example, that of the Bernoulli numbers, she recognises the need for 'cycles of cycles'. She includes a large table tracing the history of the 24 variables needed for computation up to a certain point. There is also a clear recognition that a good notation is important and that mathematical notation is insufficient. (Davies: 'Her notes have a surprisingly "modern" feeling when compared to anything Menabrea wrote, and perhaps Babbage also.')

There were female mathematicians before Ada Lovelace (Hypatia, for example, was a skilled mathematician, mainly remembered for being torn to pieces for impiety by the early Christians). Lovelace, however — after whom a modern computer language (ADA) is named — was the first woman to contribute significantly to the development of computer science.

If Ada Lovelace is one household name, at least in computer circles, then Grace Murray Hopper is another. Born in 1906, she attended Yale University (MA in 1930, PhD in 1934). After becoming an associate professor at Vassar, she joined the US Navy in December 1943 and was ordered to the Bureau of Ordnance Computation Project at Harvard: "I didn't know what to expect. I walked into a room and Professor Howard Aiken said, 'Lieutenant, that is a calculating machine'. I looked at the monstrous device stretching 51 feet across a large room. It was Mark I, and I was stepping into history."

In 1949, Commander Hopper joined the Eckert-Mauchley Computer Corporation as the senior mathematician, and stayed with the company as senior programmer when it was bought by the Remington Rand Corporation. She rose to a position roughly equivalent to that of vice-president. As Director of Automatic Programming she published, in 1952, the first paper on compilers. In the subsequent years she published well over fifty papers on software and programming languages. With a strong interest in COBOL, she attended the first meeting of CODASYL, and has also served on the ANSI X3.4 Committee on the standardisation of computer languages and became a member of the CODASYL Executive Committee. In 1973 she was promoted to the rank of captain in the US Navy, and throughout the 1960s and 1970s received a host of awards — including the Data Processing Management Association (DPMA) 'Man of the Year' award in 1969.

Dr Grace Hopper has long regarded the data processing world as one of the best business environments for women, pointing out that in the US about one third of all programmers are women. She has argued that, as a young industry, data processing has no long-established traditions of prejudice against women in employment. (In 1969 the US Navy had nine women captains, three of whom were in data processing.)

At the same time, Grace Hopper is less than sympathetic to the women's liberation movement. She has described the movement as 'tommyrot and nonsense' — 'If you want to do something you can do it. Being a woman won't hold you back, if you have the desire, the courage and the skills.' She observed that women were active in many jobs during the war, but afterwards 'most of them elected to go back to being housewives ... most of the girls preferred to return to a traditional feminine role.' It is assumed that everyone is responsible for themselves as individuals ('Everyone is given opportunities to make decisions about the direction his life will take. I decided early upon a career, not a family'). Many feminists would be keen to point out that this is not a choice that confronts most men. It is generally taken for granted that a man will opt for both career *and* family.

In the early days of computing it was inevitable that there were very few computer specialists (Hopper: 'Do you realize that in the late nineteen-forties you could have put all the computer people in one small room'). As the industry developed, the number of computer specialists — including women — increased to the point where it no longer seemed anomalous to find women occupying any particular computing post, even though they remained relatively rare in dp management and other senior positions.

Some women have developed business activities in computing. For example, (Mrs) Steve Shirley, after designing software for an ICL subsidiary, founded F International Ltd (at first Freelance Programmers Ltd) in 1962. One aim was to help women at home to continue to work efficiently and satisfactorily. Originally designed for women, F International* now employs several men, and one idea proposed by a member of the organisation is that she and her husband be treated as one working unit.

F International provides consultancy, analysis, programming and relevant management advice to a clientele of central and local government, banks, insurance companies and financial institutions. In 1979 Steve Shirley was the first woman in computing to reach the finals of the Business Woman of the Year Award, sponsored by *The Times* and Veuve Clicquot Champagne. For example, she is Vice President (Professional) of the British Computer Society (BCS), and chairs the Computing Group of the Computers, Systems and Electronics Requirements Board.

By 1970 it was possible to profile a number of women who had progressed significantly in the data processing industry. For example, Jill Smedley, in 'A Sex by Themselves' (*Data Systems*, June 1970) gives details of the careers of such women as:

— Grace Hopper (see above);

* See also Chapter 5.

- Miriam Stephenson (then Commercial Contracts Manager at the US National Data Processing Service — ('I have reached higher than any other woman in NDPS but that's probably due to age and experience');

- Cherry Lewis (then at Freelance Programmers) — ('In general I feel that women make better programmers than men but men make better analysts — they're better at design and creativity work somehow. A woman will write a straightforward program whereas a man will add loops to save seconds');

- Gillian Charmer (then responsible for Quality Control at Software Sciences). She has observed that secretaries don't know how to react with a woman boss ('they stop talking when I come into the room — or if they are talking about knitting patterns or something they carry on'). And in her view, women prefer to have their job defined ('in general they're not decision makers');

- Estelle Mendoza (then Managing Director of 1900 Recruitment Ltd) — ('I have very few jobs in higher management for women. There are chances in consultancy and lots in programming — but management ...'). One problem was the UK legislative situation in 1970 (largely unchanged today): a woman was not allowed to do night shift work without another woman present. And Mendoza often heard the (male) employer comment that 'women will marry and leave us';

- Joyce McDonald-Ross (then Project Leader at the Chelsea and Kensington Hospitals scheme, formerly General Manager at SCAN). She has observed that employers 'seem happier to keep their women on the technical side — definitely don't like them in general management';

- Steve Shirley (see above and also Chapter 5).

Since 1970 there has been uneven development in the position of women in computing. The outstanding successful women have consolidated and advanced their positions, but it is still rare to find female dp managers or female computing executives. Some women achieve 'man-of-the-year' awards, which many feminists may see as at least ironical. We have already seen that Grace

Hopper won the 1969 Data Processing Management Association (DPMA), Computer Sciences 'Man-of-the-Year' Award. In 1979, Dr Ruth Davis won the same award.

Ruth Davis programmed three of the first digital computers (SEAC, ORDVAC and UNIVAC I), and she has worked for the US Navy, the Lister Hill National Centre for Biomedical Communication, the US National Bureau of Standards, and the US Department of Defense. She was responsible for the first robotics programme in the Department of Defense, and sponsored the famous 'Shakey' robot at SRI International. Her degrees (BA, MA and PhD, *summa cum laude*) have been followed by an Honorary Doctorate (Carnegie Mellon University) and other awards.

In the UK a number of highly successful women had made important contributions to computing by the late 1970s (we have already mentioned Steve Shirley). Pam Morton is director of an advanced computer studies course at Thames Polytechnic, and believes that women make especially good systems analysts and designers. They have an exciting future in computing because they are better at it than men. One in seven of her students are female and 'more often than not, girls beat men hands down' (*Watford Echo*, 16/1/76). It is suggested that communication, so important in computer work, seems to come more naturally to women, as does project management.

Though women are poorly represented in management, their contributions are obvious here, as elsewhere. Jan Roberts is manager of systems and data processing at British International Paper, and Marion Lewis organised the installation of a computer at Barts Hospital, London. Jane Pugh is managing the London Science Museum's computing gallery, in addition to her other studies. Clearly women can make extremely successful managers in computing as they can in other fields.

It is obvious that there are outstanding women in the computer industry, though numerically women are under-represented as one ascends academic, government and company hierarchies. It should be emphasised that the circumstance of female high-achievers in data processing does not signal a situation of equal opportunity in the industry. Some of the factors that relate to discrimination, and the consequent constraints on the proper advancement of women in computing, are discussed in Chapters 2 and 3.

MEDIA ATTITUDES

It is worth concluding the present background chapter with a brief indication that demeaning images of women are still presented in data processing publications. Much of this type of media material is concerned with advertising. One can debate its importance but certain conclusions seem inescapable:

— Where women are presented as 'decorative adjuncts' in advertisements for equipment or other products, this inevitably reinforces the sexual image of women at the possible expense of their creative or intellectual qualities. This in turn makes it more difficult — for both men and women — to see female potential as highly relevant to every level of activity in the data processing, or any other, industry;

— A large number of women are repelled by stereotyped media images. This situation can be seen as highly discouraging to ambitious women who expect career advancement by virtue of their relevant personal qualities;

— The use of women as decorative packages for equipment and other products in advertisements may be commercially unnecessary. It can also be counter-productive in circumstances of increasing sensitivity to the social requirements for sexual equality in the modern world.

It is not always realised how extensively women have been used in technical publications to sell products. A decade ago the author briefly scanned a range of journals. At that time, pictures of women in bikinis (or nothing at all) were being used to advertise a wide range of industrial products, from Simplicity Elm Mild Steel Tube to Ashley Wall Switches, from Airking Air Conditioners to Spiral Tube Air Blast Coolers. Gelb used to advertise their chemical reactors and other chemical equipment by means of a monthly 'Gelb Girl', usually clad in a bikini, who appeared in the journal *Chemical Engineering*. Lipton Fork Lift Hire used to employ a different girl (sketched — not photographed) from one advertisement to another.

Over the last decade the advertising policy of publications has scarcely been affected by the impact of the women's movement. Nor is it illegal to publish advertisements which may be recognised as sexist, and the Advertising Standards Authority is quite likely to reject claims by trade unions, the Equal Opportunities Commission and private individuals that particular advertisements are offensive or demeaning to women. Examples are given in a recent ASA report (published late-1980) of complaints about sexist advertising that have been turned down: where pictures of scantily-dressed women were used with suggestive captions to advertise carpets, tights and record cartridges. It is noted that six per cent of complaints to the ASA concern sexism, and that this is 'a matter of concern'. The ASA is running a campaign in 1981 to investigate the extent to which women are offended by sexist advertising.

In computing and data processing publications there are frequent examples of this sort of advertising. Particular journals and particular manufacturers can clearly be seen to be associated with such material. It is worth giving a few examples (without affording publicity to journals or equipment suppliers):

— A picture of an apparently naked woman, plus a caption ('The Naked Truth! There's nothing to hide in the way we operate'), is used to advertise contract specialists in the computer field — an unusual advertisement in that the female model is acknowledged by name;

— A picture of a woman in a bikini, plus a caption ('The Squeesable One'), is used to advertise a fully expandable multiplexer;

— A picture of a seated woman, plus a caption ('The body's beautiful, but you'll love your... for her mind'), is used to advertise a microcomputer;

— A picture of a seated woman wearing what looks like a leotard, high-heeled shoes and wings (!), plus a caption making reference to 'Your Guardian Angel', is used to advertise miniature relays;

— A picture of an apparently naked woman, tied up with masses of cord, plus a caption ('... doing 5 to 10 on a bum wrap'), is used to advertise LSI adapter boards, ECL logic boards, LED display sockets, etc.

Sometimes a deliberately unattractive woman is used for advertising purposes. In one instance, a gap-toothed woman with rollers in her hair (caption: 'We never said they'd be good-looking'), is used to advertise switching power supplies. In another advertisement, a lingerie clad woman, plus caption ('How's your love life?'), is used to sell a computer game. At least in this case the woman and caption are seemingly relevant to the character of the product in question.

Posters too may exploit women for commercial purposes. For example, a poster designed in Germany — showing an ill-clad woman holding a microcomputer in front of her — is being freely handed out to UK dealers. At least one woman objected strongly to the poster on display at the 1980 Personal Computer World exhibition. And objections to what is taken to be sexist material are often printed in the letter columns of the computer journals. For example:

- 'Congratulations on the 'exposing' of certain advertising practices which capitalise on a woman's peripherals to sell a product... although it might be argued that the photograph of a woman breast-feeding has artistic value, the headline, 'The milking of micro kindness' is, at best, extremely questionable taste' (Joanne Matteucci);

- 'I find myself pondering your sincerity when I turn.... to read your article on reprographics. The use of a sparsely-clad woman, *without a head* (italics in original), I find disgusting, and it is this type of illustration which will continue to support the myth of the 'submissive, decorative' woman' (D T C Wiersma);

- 'I take exception to the advertisement... showing an apparently naked lady (?) atop a small business system' (Mrs J B Howells);

- 'What a pity that a serious computer journal should accept an advertisement such as the one... There can be no possible justification for printing a completely irrelevant picture of a naked woman sitting beside a terminal' (Joanna Hunter).

At least one man felt compelled to reply to some of these comments. He talked about 'grim humourless female libbers' but felt unable to allow his name and address to be published.

Another seemingly sexist ploy is to demean women in cartoon. One of the complaints rejected by the ASA concerned a cartoon strip showing a salesman being seduced by a housewife clad only in underwear (and this to sell carpets!). Cartoons in computer periodicals often relate to the physical characteristics of women or to their supposed stupidity. Hence, in one cartoon, one man remarks to another, about a passing overweight woman, 'We like to think of Miss Melchoir as the mainframe of the typing pool...' In another cartoon, a shapely woman earns the male comment: 'She should worry about automation. I can't see a silicon chip replacing her.' In yet another, one woman at a terminal says to another, 'Basic, Fortran, Cobol, APL — it's all Greek to me!'

Sometimes, for reasons best known to themselves, a computer. company may publish eccentric or patronising material on women. For instance, the Motorola Communications Group (Free Trade Zone, Bayan Lepas, Penang) published, alongside a drawing of a test-tube, a *Chemical Analysis of Women* (Figure 1).

Whatever one's reaction to the Motorola 'Chemical Analysis', it is unambiguous, blatant, with 'high visibility'. However, many aspects of the media treatment of women are implicit and unobtrusive. There are points that are unimportant but which can be debated. For example, in profiling new staff appointments, a journal may introduce people by both first name and surname, thereafter referring to men by their surnames (implying respect) but to women by their first names (implying friendliness, intimacy)

The use of pronouns in computer textbooks is also significant. It is assumed that where a pronoun is required, 'he' will be used, thus reinforcing the idea that we should expect computer staff to be male. Sometimes there is explicit stereotyping, as in Dennis Carlyle's *Careers in Computing*, where reasons are given why data preparation is a particularly suitable 'profession' for girls. The firm impression is created that girls do not, and should not, aim at anything beyond data control. ('This alone is sufficient reason for not placing this book in the hands of boys or girls, since it promotes precisely those sex stereotypes which one is hoping to eradicate' — Angela Arratoon, careers officer with the Inner London Education Authority.)

Symbol:	Occurrence:
WOE	Found wherever men exist

Physical Properties:

Very active — Boil at nothing and may freeze any minute. Melt when properly treated. Very bitter if not well used. Great pretenders. Where spreading of news and incidents are concerned, they are better than BBC.

Chemical Properties:

Very active. Possess great affinity for gold and precious stone. Very choosy. Violent reaction when left alone. Able to absorb great amounts of expensive food and clothing. Turn green when placed beside better looking specimens. Age rapidly. Possess the best accessories which men like most.

Uses:

Highly ornamental. Useful as a tonic in acceleration if in low spirits, etc. Equalise distribution of wealth. Are probably the most powerful (income) reducing agent.

Caution:

Highly explosive when in experienced hands.

Figure 1

A recent *Computing* (4/10/79) profile of Carole Langley, the female manager of the Liverpool Stock Exchange, provoked correspondence. A man, Laurence Beckreck, observed that much less space had been given to the item than to a profile of a *man* on the same page, and that the approach to the two people was completely different — no mention was made of *his* marital status, dating arrangements or outside hobbies. Again there is the clear impression that a woman is being treated less seriously as a *professional* person than a man would be. And Beckreck was suitably applauded for his enlightened attitudes — 'Roll on the day when all men in dp share his attitudes..' (Ruth McCullough).

There are other approaches that reveal male prejudice, or perhaps ignorance. For example, there is the assumption (see *Computer Weekly*, 23/10/80) that 'women have nearly made it', that the battle is nearly won. Hence the CW comment in response to the ASTMS pamphlet, *Computer Professionals, Image and Reality* – 'Come on, ASTMS! Apart from the "related area of telecommunications" which may well employ a mere handful of women, DP is the one field where many women have succeeded.' This is true but it says little about the ratios of men and women in the different types of computer jobs.

Finally we should comment briefly on the bogus feminism that characterises some male (and female) attitudes. Sometimes women find themselves being encouraged in a patronising way, because 'they have something unique to offer' to the computing industry. For instance, Mike Cooley of Lucas Aerospace has suggested (*Computing*, 9/10/80) that predominantly male values have raped science and technology for too long – 'It would be an enormous political and philosophical contribution to society if more women were to come into science and technology... to challenge the 'male' values that have distorted 'science' for too long. It would be a contribution, not only to women's liberation and that of humanity as a whole, but also towards a science which is more caring, liberatory, socially relevant and which enhances our naturalness.' This appears progressive but is basically unsound. It does in fact enshrine sexist attitudes, where traditional prejudice about women is given a false gloss. What is required is quite simple – that men and women be given a chance to do a job on a basis of equality.

SUMMARY

The position of women in computing cannot be divorced from their overall position in employment and from the broader attitudes in society. Women tend to find themselves in a few industry categories, and these tend to be relatively low-grade in status. At the same time there is some indication that traditional prejudice is less significant in data processing, a relatively new industry. Many highly competent women have progressed far in a wide range of computer organisations (in government, commerce, industry and the academic world). However, such success stories do not demonstrate that a broad situation of equal opportunity exists for men and women in data processing. There is evidence that girls are still discouraged from taking scientific and technical subjects in schools, and from the practical and manipulative activities that would prepare them most suitably for an engineering career.

There is also evidence that women are presented in a trivial or demeaning way in some data processing publications, and that this circumstance can be irritating or discouraging to many women hoping to make a career in the industry. At the same time, some women argue that (for example) the 'decorative' use of women in advertising is inconsequential and that the important considerations are that women be given equal educational and employment opportunities. Feminists would argue that a demeaning presentation of women in the media can only retard any movement towards educational and employment equality, and that women can only make effective progress if all the relevant areas are tackled at the same time.

Discrimination against women exists in the data processing industries of the US, Europe and elsewhere (see Chapters 2 and 3), but it is possible to debate the reasons and its extent. For reasons of educational discrimination, women may come to computing less equipped than their male counterparts, and may then be treated on their (artificially inferior) merits by an industry less affected than others by traditional prejudice. It is certainly true that as one ascends the hierarchies of computer organisations (government departments, university faculties, companies), women are progressively less well represented, though there are different (and characteristic) patterns from one type of organisation to another.

The circumstance of economic recession — coupled with government policies aimed at reducing public expenditure (on education, industrial investment, etc) — may be seen as making the woman's position in computing, as elsewhere, more difficult. There may well be more constraints on educational progress and fewer employment opportunities (there is evidence that recessions hit women harder than men). However, significant progress has been made — in legislation, employment policies, and social attitudes. It is realistic to believe that changes in these areas reflect a heightened sensitivity to the position of women in society, and that this will have important consequences for the computer industry in the years to come.

2 Equality or Discrimination?

INTRODUCTION

The circumstances of employment inequalities between men and women can be interpreted in many ways. There is evidence that women seeking jobs, or in employment, are treated differently to men, and that the various modes of discrimination place artificial constraints on female career development. Much of the discrimination, where it exists, in industry in general and data processing in particular, reflects traditional prejudices in the broader culture — and we are assuming that such attitudes are ill-founded and should be discouraged. At the same time it is necessary to mention an interpretation of employment inequalities which suggests that, to some extent, women themselves are to blame.

Many observers, men and women have argued that 'women are their own worst enemies' in the way they strive for justice and emancipation. It is suggested that women are often 'strident' or 'hysterical' in pressing their case, and that this is counter-productive, alienating potential allies and delaying legitimate social change. Such comments often disguise a broad satisfaction with prevailing social patterns, even where these enshrine manifest injustice.

Sometimes successful women in computing (and elsewhere) are indifferent, or even hostile, to the efforts of the women's movement. (One writer has dubbed such attitudes the 'Queen Bee syndrome' — 'I worked long and hard to get here; why should she have it any easier?'.) To some extent this indicates how women themselves can be influenced by a sexist culture, prepared to accept traditional values that may limit the development of women in society. This circumstance is relevant to computing, as

41

it is to other fields. For example, at a session on women in computing at the 1980 US National Computer Conference, Ida Mason
(LeHigh University) suggested that female attitudes were a significant bar to the advancement of women — she advised women to
'forget past prejudices and face real time problems in the world.'
One of the problems is that responsible positions involve travel,
and city travel at night can be dangerous for a woman: if she travels with male colleagues there is often criticism from their wives.
Another problem is that female employers and managers may
themselves incline to discriminate against women (Ida Mason — 'A
woman faced with job candidates will tend to choose the man
rather than the woman, in the same way as users tend to choose
IBM, because it's safe.')

Women's attitudes are obviously highly relevant to the progress
of women in society. Where some women appear shrill or strident,
this is generally in response to perceived prejudice and the inertia
of social institutions. Where some women, professionally successful or not, share traditional sexist prejudices this highlights a situation of competing social ideas rather than a simple male/female
divide. In any event it is necessary to explore the character of discrimination and the various mechanisms by which it is sustained or
eroded.

STEREOTYPING

A common feminist complaint is that distorted assumptions are
made about women, ie people allow their judgements to be affected by 'stereotypes' — inaccurate, demeaning and inflexible images
of what women are, what they expect, what they can achieve, etc.
The complaint is justified (see sections below), and it is important
to understand how stereotypes occur and how they reinforce traditional social patterns.

The stereotype encourages the use of simplistic labels and dis-
courages cautious reflection that may disturb established views.
There are male stereotypes as well as female, but in male-dominated society *male* stereotypes are not allowed to undermine the
rich imagery that describes male potential. By contrast there are
some special pressures that encourage the idea that *female* stereotypes define the sum-total of female potential. There is already

evidence of the negative impact of sex-role stereotyping on personnel selection and perceptions of ability (see bibliography in Schein, 1978): for example, in one study of several hundred managers (male and female) it was found that for both male and female respondents, to 'think manager' meant to 'think male'.

Where discrimination exists in the data processing industry there can be no doubt that stereotyping is a contributory cause, likely to affect the treatment of women at every stage of their career development – from early education, through job appointments and company training schemes, to promotion to the higher echelons of an organisation. In a recent study (Woodruff, 1980), the personalities of 202 data processing staff were scrutinised, and males and females were found to possess remarkably similar personality profiles:

Perhaps the most interesting study finding was that the personality needs profiles of DP males and females are amazingly *similar* (original italics). This may offer some insight into the belief that female employees present proportionally as many problems as male employees, and often the same basic problems.

Such work helps to undermine simple stereotyping. There are no easy labels that can be differentially applied to females and males in most employment situations. Where efforts are made to evaluate staff potential in data processing, as in other industries, people should be assessed as individuals. In most organisations, management would claim to work on this basis. There is, nonetheless, plenty of evidence of the negative impact of stereotypical thinking in most organisations where the relevant research has been carried out.

LEGISLATION

Many countries have enacted legislation to advance the position of women in employment and other areas of society. In the UK, the Equal Pay Act, passed in 1970, came into effect in 1975, when the Sex Discrimination Act also came into operation. Many observers suggested that, though such legislation represented a considerable advance, people should not expect utopian, 'overnight' changes in employment practices. It was recognised that the new laws related to deep-seated attitudes consolidated over centuries, and that even if (for example), educational discrimination were to cease abruptly, the consequences would take many years to work through the employment environment.

The *novelty* of equal-rights legislation has also led to difficulties in interpretation. There have been arguments about the precise application of the statutory rules to particular employment cases, with consequent delays in settling claims or anomalies. One purpose of the Equal Opportunities Commission (EOC), established by the legislation, is to review the working of the Acts. Wainwright (1979) has pointed out that it would be surprising if EOC reviews 'failed to reveal some aspects of the legislation which did not require technical amendment to remove anomalies or fill loopholes created by drafting errors or erroneous decisions.'

The UK, and other EEC countries, are also affected by European Economic Community law, some of which is directly enforceable in UK courts. EEC provisions are generally seen as useful in interpreting national legislation in member countries, the assumption being that the relevant parliaments must, when legislating, comply with the obligations to the Community.

For purposes of achieving (or safeguarding) equality between men and women, European law comprises the provisions of the Treaty of Rome, Regulations, and Directives. Article 119 of the Treaty declares that: 'each Member State shall.... ensure and subsequently maintain the principle that men and women should receive equal pay for equal work.' (*Equal* work was originally defined, in the Article, as the *same* work, but a later Directive has stipulated that the principle also applies to work 'to which equal value is attributed.')

Another EEC Directive declares that Member States should implement the principle of equal treatment for men and women as regards access to employment, and that this means 'that there shall be no discrimination whatsoever on grounds of sex either directly or indirectly' (although certain exceptions to the rule are also indicated). The requirements are broadly met in the UK by the provisions of the Equal Pay Act and the Sex Discrimination Act. However, it was announced in March 1979 (reported in *Department of Employment Gazette*, April 1979) that the UK was one of seven Member States against whom the EEC Commission intended to initiate proceedings for failing to observe fully the equal pay Directive.

There is also growing sensitivity in the United States to the rights of women in employment and elsewhere. In fact, though still regarded as inadequate by many observers, American law can help to guide the interpretation of UK anti-discrimination legislation. The judgements of US courts have no authority in the UK, but UK judges will sometimes quote American experience when formulating decisions. A key American achievement was the formulation of an Equal Rights Amendment (ERA) to the US constitution. In the enthusiastic early seventies the passage of this constitutional amendment seemed guaranteed.

The ERA, like many equal rights provisions in the US and elsewhere, was first formulated more than half-a-century ago. In 1971 it passed through the House of Representatives by a 354 to 24 vote, and went through the Senate with only eight opposing votes. The proposed amendment − 'Equality of rights under the law shall not be denied or abridged by the US or any State on account of sex' − requires ratification by three quarters of all States once Congress have approved it. The failure, to date, to achieve this ratification has been interpreted by some observers as evidence of the diminishing impact of the women's movement in the US.

There is an international awareness of the need for legislation to advance the position of women in employment and other areas of social life. Even a brief survey of the literature shows a similar awareness in many disparate countries: for example, the USSR (Biryukova, 1980), Hungary (Gomori, 1980), the Nordic countries (Nielson, 1980), the Netherlands (*Eur.Ind.Relat.Revs*, Nos 62 and 75, see bibliography), Ireland (Eur.Ind.Relat.Rev, No 43, see bibliography), and Australia (Connell, 1980). In these circumstances it must be acknowledged that, at least in terms of legislation, women's rights are being progressively enshrined in the fabric of national states.

EMPLOYMENT IN GENERAL

There is a naive view that where there is a special injustice it is sufficient to pass a law. Some people felt that female inequality in the UK would be quite adequately dealt with by the Sex Discrimination Act and the Equal Pay Act. There was confidence that the Equal Opportunities Commission, established as a statutory body, would quickly ensure that the legislation would eliminate sex discrimination and promote equal opportunities. In fact, half-a-decade after introducing legislation there appear to be few changes as a result of the law.

One possible index of the effectiveness of legislation is the extent to which law is invoked by those it is intended to defend. In fact in the first three years of the Acts being in operation only 310 individuals had taken cases to an Industrial Tribunal under the provisions of the Sex Discrimination Act. This compared with more than 1300 people under the Equal Pay Act. These figures may seem substantial until it is realised that, over a five-year period, more than 35,000 men and women have taken cases under the unfair dismissal provisions of the Employment Protection Act and the Trade Union and Labour Relations Act. And successes of individual complaints have been low under the Sex Discrimination and Equal Pay Acts (16 per cent and 33 per cent respectively).

These facts, without further information, admit of more than one interpretation. It may be argued that the little usage of the laws only shows that discrimination against women is not widespread and that injustice is minimal. Other explanations may relate to women's lack of awareness of statutory provisions, and to most people's reluctance to take a grievance to court. It is significant that some employers have declared an intention to continue discriminating against women, or men, despite the new laws.

In a research project conducted by the London School of Economics, focussing on 26 organisations, it was found that the legislative impact of the Sex Discrimination Act was very limited (see bibliography). The Act had caused few practices to change, and the detectable changes were superficial. There was a general assumption that existing policies met the requirements of the law and provided equal opportunities for men and women. Overt discrimination was removed from recruitment advertisements, but there was little change to training and promotion procedures. Little attempt was made to develop equal opportunity policies and programmes. The LSE research suggested that the relevant legislation would be unlikely to remove detectable discrimination. Four findings were particularly revealing:

- In 22 of the 26 organisations investigated, one or more managers concerned with appointing staff, training or promotion declared that they were practising discrimination against women (or men) and intended to do so in future;

- Most employers who took action under the initial impact of the Act thought that everything necessary had been done, and that no further action was required;

- Many practices and attitudes were detected which limited women's opportunities. Some criteria, such as hours of work and lifting, were sometimes legitimate but more often reflected tradition and male career patterns;

- Policies for anti-discrimination and equal opportunities were generally regarded by employers as low-priority issues, both when considered in the context of other employment legislation and in the context of the prevailing economic climate. Nor did there appear to be much grass-roots pressure for change from trade unions or from women themselves.

It has been argued by many observers (eg Glucklich and Povall, 1979) that organisations should take into account recent legal developments — both to protect themselves from potential grievances and to improve company morale and efficiency. Some important legal decisions have emanated from the Employment Appeal Tribunal (EAT) and the Court of Appeal. In two particular cases — those of Linda Price and Letitia Steel — the Employment Appeal Tribunal interpreted the Sex Discrimination Act provisions relating to indirect discrimination (see also Wainwright, 1979, Chapter 5). The employers concerned failed to convince the tribunals that the criteria (an age limit of 28 in the case of Price, and seniority as a criterion for allocation to a preferred type of work in the case of Steel) were justified by the *necessity* rather than by the *convenience* of the business.

These are important findings. Few organisations regularly review all job and person specifications to ensure that the prevailing criteria are justifiable. *Un*justifiable criteria can be a source of unlawful discrimination.

Attitudes of employers and managers are obviously crucial in any anti-discrimination and equal-opportunities programmes. One early (1973) survey revealed attitudes to the impending Equal Pay and Sex Discrimination Acts (Hunt, 1975). The study took a sample of organisations with 100 or more employees from the main industries employing women: information was collected on personnel practices in 398 organisations, and on the attitudes of those people who provided the information. Specific subjects were examined in connection with attitudes to equal opportunity.

It was found that 75.8 per cent of the (mostly male) formulators of policy, and 81.9 per cent of the (mostly male) implementers of policy had serious reservations about equal pay. It was suggested that it would become harder for women to get work (since women cannot or will not work the same hours); that women are a less stable part of the workforce; that it would affect family life; that women cannot do the same work; that men should earn more; and that the cost to employers would be too great. Despite these 'serious reservations', a majority of the interviewees declared themselves unreservedly in favour of equal pay. However, the enthusiasm for equal pay diminished with the increasing size of the establishment and increasing numbers of women employed.

The study also examined why few women rise to senior positions or do skilled work. A majority of the policy formulators and implementers tended to blame women themselves, suggesting that the explanation lay in the choices that women make. It was said that women were not career-conscious, that they were unwilling to train, unreliable and less able to accept responsibility because of their family duties. Only a minority of the interviewees thought it would be a good thing if more women rose to senior posts, but two thirds were prepared to concede that more women should be trained for highly skilled work.

A key finding was the prejudice that surrounded the recruitment of women. When those with responsibility for recruitment were asked about required qualities in candidates, a majority of interviewees thought that any attribute was more likely to be found in men. When asked whether they would choose a man or a woman if both had the same qualities, the only jobs for which a majority would choose a woman were catering or domestic work.

Table 2 shows the reasons given for preferring men in 601 cases of the study. The conclusion for this survey appears to be unambiguous: 'Most of those responsible for the recruitment of employees start off with the belief that a woman applicant is likely to be inferior to a man in all the qualities that are important for selection. It seems highly unlikely that legislation would change such a belief – certainly not within a few years' (Wainwright, 1979, p 22).

Reasons for preferring a man	Policy implementers who are more likely to engage men	
	601	%
Physical reasons		32.8
Get longer service from a man		12.3
Hours unsuitable, overtime, weekends		10.5
Dirty job, physical conditions bad		8.5
Women cannot control men		7.9
Women would hear bad language		6.2
Employees would rather work for a man		5.3
Women are less adaptable		2.3
Dangerous job		2.1
Unions would object		1.2
Women not allowed to work nightshift		0.7
'Always been a man's job'		32.3
Other reasons		4.9
Vague, no reason given		3.1

Table 2   Reasons for Preferring to Employ a Man (Source: Hunt A, 1975)

The survey also showed that sixty-three per cent of those responsible for formulating personnel policy thought that there were some jobs that no woman could do, whereas only fourteen per cent reckoned that there were some jobs that no man could do. The nature of the beliefs is evident when the jobs for which women are said to be unsuitable are examined. It is also clear that men were thought to be unable to do those jobs with low status.

The most common reason for supposing that no women could do particular jobs was physical effort, though some of the jobs were performed by women in war-time. (The well-documented history of 19th-Century women in mines may also be taken as relevant.) The reason that 'it has always been a man's job' illuminates the traditional attitudes to women and work.

In a detailed US survey (R & D Monograph 65, 1978; see bibliography), produced for the Employment and Training Administration, US Department of Labour, many of the findings are similar to those in UK research. The US study examined the position of women ('in traditionally male jobs') in ten public utility companies. Despite evident problems faced by women, considerable sympathy for equality for women in employment was recorded. The following are verbatim extracts from the ten-page Summary of Findings:

- *The experiences of the 10 companies in their efforts to integrate women into traditionally-male jobs have been considerably more positive than negative.* Not unexpectedly, the companies have encountered some serious problems in working towards the goal of achieving equal opportunities for male and female employees. Negative attitudes as well as both overt and covert resistance were revealed, and some performance failures proved to be costly to both the women involved and the companies. Nonetheless, if all the forces that might be expected to work against successful integration were taken into account, the results will seem to be remarkably successful;

- *A great majority of the women in traditionally-male jobs were judged by their managers, peers, and subordinates to be performing at least as well as most men in the respective jobs.* In considering this performance record, it must be remembered that most of the women had been in their new jobs a relatively short time;

- *Significantly, however, there was evidence that the target women had to be performing better than most men in order to earn a rating of 'good' or 'excellent';*

- *In most of the 10 companies studied there appeared to be a a positive commitment to the principle of equal opportunity for women among the majority of persons in the management ranks.* Even those managers who found it difficult to accept the changing role of women in the workforce usually accepted their responsibility to live up to the spirit and the letter of the equal opportunity laws;

— *Like those of the majority of managers, the attitudes of male peers of the target woman were decidedly more positive than negative.* Again, however, the peers of women in white-collar male-oriented jobs had much more positive feelings about their female working colleagues than did peers of women in blue-collar jobs. *Indeed, many of the women entering blue-collar jobs experienced some degree of harassment from male peers, serious enough in some cases to impede the women's work;*

— *There was evidence to show that pay discrimination in the companies studied was probably less significant than has been the case in most companies in the past.* Fewer than five per cent of the women thought that they were definitely being paid less than men of comparable background and experience in their jobs....

A study published in October 1980 by the UK Industrial Society focusses on the employment of highly qualified women in manufacturing industry. Some of the findings are highly relevant to the data processing industry. It is found, for example, that there are very few highly qualified women currently employed in industry sectors requiring technical qualifications. Where women *are* employed in industry this is usually outside the mainstream career path or line management. Also, highly qualified women tend to prefer careers with service industries and the public sector.

A general conclusion is that the position of women in UK industry is unlikely to improve significantly unless positive steps are taken in schools and companies. For example, steps should be taken to influence the subject choice of girls, and companies could develop career paths into management from the various support functions in which women are employed.

Most companies would claim that active steps to advance the position of women are unnecessary, that prevailing non-discriminatory personnel policies are adequate. However, a few companies have tried to create a specific policy for women employees. It is worth mentioning the efforts of one such company.

Rank Xerox is a multinational company engaged in the manufacture and marketing of electrostatic reprographic equipment.
The firm employs well over 30,000 and has operating companies
around the world. The personnel policies in Rank Xerox have been
traditionally developed at individual operating company level so
that they can be adapted to local circumstances. However, when
top management committed to equal opportunities, decided on a
policy statement in this field, they felt it should be developed at
international, rather than national, level.

In 1973 a high-level working party was set up with the remit to
'establish a policy for the employment of women within the company'. Information was obtained, via an eight-page questionnaire,
from all the operating companies. National statistics were com-
piled on the female working populations, and company statistics
were obtained on female employees, their marital status, job categories, etc (specific questions were asked about company experience in recruiting and retaining women in sales and service).
Efforts were also made to collect information on positive and negative attitudes held by managers and staff towards a policy aimed
at improving the position of women. A draft document was then
submitted to the personnel managers in all the operating companies for their comments. (Top management later decided that the
document's scope be broadened to include minorities as well as
women.)

A specific equal opportunity programme was adopted by Rank
Xerox in 1974. The commitment is based on the principle that 'it
is a business need to explore every possible source of talent, including the half of the human race which is female, and the minority
groups.' The aim of the company is to be 'a pacemaker in this
field of social equality throughout its multinational operations'.

The policy document emphasises the need for positive targets
for the employment of women, and the need to monitor progress.
It is suggested that each operating company 'should aim to have a
considerably higher proportion, compared with most companies,
of women in what have hitherto been regarded as 'male' jobs. The
companies are advised to classify employees appropriately (eg
managers, clerks, technicians, etc) and to determine the percentage

of women:

Recruitment — both internal and external job advertisements should state in heavy type that both men and women are invited to apply and that all apprenticeships and initial-entry training schemes are open to both men and women. Any case where a job must be reserved for one sex has to be agreed by the personnel manager. All recruitment booklets are required to spell out the equal opportunity policy, and women-only educational establishments are included in recruitment visits. Public relations departments are encouraged to publicise the equal opportunity policy and programme as much as possible.

Management — managers are advised that the attainment of the policy objectives on the employment of women 'is as important as any other traditional business responsibility', that 'full account of performance will be taken in all future performance reviews', and that appraisal documents should include this requirement. Also managerial job descriptions should include the requirement to 'develop the employment of women, particularly in sales, service, specialist, professional and management posts.'

Promotion — personnel managers are required to 'review personally the appraisals and development plans for all women above clerical grades, and those within clerical grades identified as having promotion potential'. And senior managers are required 'to identify a number of suitable development posts for women in this area,' and to 'identify individual women within the company, who have educational qualifications or high intelligence and the desire to attempt an executive career.' The manager should then take steps to 'tailor training and development packages for those identified individuals'.

Pay — personnel managers are asked 'to check that the interpretation of 'equal work' is fair and is not used as a cloak for continued inequality'. It is suggested that anomalies be put right at the next pay review, and the programme encourages an analysis of pay levels and pay awards for all non-clerical female staff.

A survey of Rank Xerox (UK) in July 1976 showed that 48 women were employed in sales, comprising 6.5 per cent of direct selling employees in the company. A target of 10 per cent for female sales staff was set for January 1977: by that time there were in fact 78 female sales staff employed, constituting 8.8 per cent of the direct sales force. In February 1977 new targets were set, for realisation by 31st October 1977. A job advertisement in *Cosmopolitan* produced 105 women applicants out of a total of 120 replies.

Internationally, Rank Xerox has achieved various successes in encouraging an improvement in the employment position of women. For example, the West German company has made positive efforts to encourage women to take up apprenticeships, and the first female refurbishing engineer qualified some years ago. The Italian company which had no female sales staff in 1973, now has women comprising around 30 per cent of the sales force. And women are reaching the higher levels of management. By 1977 the Norwegian Rank Xerox company had a female manager reporting directly to the chief executive of the operating company, and the French company had three third-line female managers.

The Rank Xerox successes show what can be achieved when senior management is committed to equal opportunities and when suitable data is available. There are lessons here for other companies.

DATA PROCESSING INDUSTRY

General

There is debate as to the extent of discrimination (against women) in the data processing industry. Some observers, rightly sensitive to any manifestation of injustice, suggest that this industry is no different to any other, that discrimination is widespread and deep-seated. Others point out that data processing is a new industry, that it emerged at a time when society was becoming increasingly aware of legitimate feminist claims. In this latter interpretation, data processing is regarded as largely emancipated from traditional prejudices about the employment of women. (A certain lecturer, Charles P Hecht, has been quoted as saying in the US, ten years ago − 'Well, gentlemen, in my opinion data processing is a plot to infuse industry with women'.)

Wherever two opposing extremes of opinion are in conflict it is a safe bet that the truth lies somewhere between them. The data processing industry may be regarded – in common with any other specialist area – as a subculture within a broader culture. In our terms, there are clear signs of discrimination but also reasonable grounds for optimism that data processing is 'flexible', less rigid than other industries where prejudice has become entrenched over many decades.

Particular Occupations

In 1973, Suzette Harold, a marketing executive of F International, surveyed the position of women in the various data processing jobs (operators, programmers, data preparation staff, systems analysts, managers, etc). A mixed situation was revealed. It is suggested that in some areas women are artificially assigned a low status, that in others female superiorities are being acknowledged, and that in yet others a broad situation of equal opportunity prevails.

Operators were seen as mostly men, though with women working alongside on a basis of equality (including night shift activities). The UK Atomic Weapons Research Establishment (Aldermaston) is instanced as a place where women worked night shifts 'as a matter of course'. When Suzette Harold tested programs at the Atomic Energy Authority's Culham laboratory, there were girl operators employed during the night shift. Then, as now, women were not prevented from taking up this kind of employment.

Data preparation staff have, for many years, been mostly women. There is no particular reason why this should be so, except for the traditional discriminatory reason that it is economically convenient for employers to shunt women into particular occupations and thereby to depress wages in that sector. (We have already seen that the Equal Pay Act cannot be invoked where the paucity of men in an occupation prevents comparison of male/female wage levels.) Where an employer's practice in maintaining low female wage rates cannot be challenged in law (or via some other effective mechanism), the employer has an obvious commercial vested interest in supporting the status quo.

Suzette Harold has suggested that women programmers are often better than men, a circumstance that has tended to overcome 'veritable mountains of prejudice' – 'I have discovered many programming managers who told me that their best programmer is a woman'. There are also suggestions that women programmers are less likely to 'job-hop' than are men.

(It is worth mentioning here that women can too easily find themselves in a Catch-22 situation. If they are barred from certain jobs, career development is stifled and women are prevented from gaining legitimate access to good salaries and high status within an organisation. If, alternatively, women are allowed into an occupation − and then, in large numbers, do extremely well in it − the occupation is in danger of becoming a 'woman's job': men are discouraged from seeking a career in that field and, by the curious mechanisms of sexist society, wages and status are depressed.)

Most UK staff employed as systems analysts, in software design and in consultancy are male, with men constituting a progressively higher proportion of staff as one ascends through the hierarchy of an organisation. There are few female data processing managers (see also Chapter 3), or female managers at any level in data processing organisations. However, here there are signs that data processing is more progressive than industry in general.

The Manufacturing Base

In manufacturing (of computers, other electronics equipment, etc) there is clear evidence of the traditional 'shunting' effect − women tend to be very heavily represented in low-grade assembly and fabrication activities, and very poorly represented in the higher echelons of manufacturing companies. The shunting of women into low-paid manufacturing work is obvious in both the developed and the under-developed world. In some countries it appears to be an avowed policy of government.

In South-East Asia, between 200,000 and 300,000 women work in electronics plants, often subsidiaries of the large semiconductor companies based in the developed world (Grossman, 1979). For example, women constitute 90 per cent of the assembly workforce in the 1400-person Intel plant in Penang, Malaysia. It is no accident that women are represented in such high numbers. Driven by the need for competitive price-cutting, the major semiconductor manufacturers have sought cheap labour to perform the labour-intensive assembly tasks essential to component manufacture. The low wages of Asian women have made possible the explosive growth in the market for semiconductor-based products.

Fairchild Camera and Instrument Company set up an assembly plant in Hong Kong in 1962, and European and Japanese companies began expanding to Hong Kong, Taiwan and South Korea. The search for ever cheaper sources of labour led the firms to Singapore (1969), Malasia (1972), Thailand (1973), and the Philippines and Indonesia (1974). A manager of a plant in Malaysia is quoted by Grossman: 'One worker working one hour produces enough to pay the wages of 10 workers working one shift plus all the cost of materials and transport.' And by 'worker' is generally meant 'woman worker'. In striving to attract foreign investment, Asian governments have emphasised the availability of masses of cheap female labour. An extract from *Malaysia: The Solid State for Electronics* (again, quoted by Grossman) asks the question, 'Who .... could be better qualified by nature and inheritance to contribute to the efficiency of a bench-assembly production line than the oriental girl?'

The need to keep wage costs down has encouraged managers of Asian plants to adopt a wide range of effective control measures. These include authoritarian discipline, the banning of trade unions, and the provision of sophisticated human relations techniques. For example, women workers in assembly plants in the Philippines are prohibited from talking on the factory floor, and are allowed only 45 minutes break time during an eight-hour shift. Workers at a Fairchild factory in Indonesia reported only being allowed a 10-minute tea break and a 15-minute lunch break.

Trade unions − organisations which might be expected to support the cause of women − are banned. If protest begins in factory plant in the Philippines, Indonesia, Thailand, Singapore, Taiwan, South Korea, etc, it is stopped by police and government officials acting within the terms of legislation prohibiting strikes in 'vital' industry (eg in foreign-owned manufacturing plant). A management representative has declared that 'Intel doesn't believe in unions,' and a semiconductor executive in California has emphasised the desirability of preventing unionisation because it would raise wages and make it harder to lay off workers.

Another consequence of unionisation would be that the health of South-East Asian women workers would come under scrutiny. Toxic fumes and eye ailments are seen as common enemies of electronics workers. Yet workers are not always informed of health hazards, and there is the suggestion (Grossman) that 'management-run health and safety committees actually divert attention from these problems'. In 1975, three years after the first electronics plant opened in Penang, nearly half the (mainly women) workers complained of worsening eyesight and frequent headaches, both conditions caused by excessive microscope work. It is expected that anyone who stays on the work for more than three years will eventually have to wear glasses — which most companies refuse to pay for.

Other dangers to women derive from caustic chemicals, all toxic and some thought to be cancer-causing. The chemicals include TCE, xylene and MEK, dangerous acids and solvents, used extensively in production. Workers are required to dip components in acids and to rub them with solvents: these activities can cause serious burns, dizziness, nausea, and in some cases fingers may be lost.

Some of the Asian problems also exist in California where hazards can arise from the chemicals used in the making of silicon wafers. About 90 per cent of the 60,000 assemblers in Silicon Valley are women, and about half are of Asian and Latin origin. Many of the women are single mothers providing the primary support for their families. Again they are often faced with unhealthy working conditions, low wages, and inadequate trade union protection. California executives work out ways of preventing unionisation and then export their refined personnel management techniques for use in subsidiary companies in South-East Asia.

It is important to consider the role of women in the manufacture of computer components throughout the world. Since a relatively small amount of such manufacture is carried out in the UK, we tend to see computer occupations as data preparation, operating, programming, systems analysis and dp management. Primary fabrication supports all these activities and bears directly on the position of women employed in the computer industry.

Discriminatory Trends and Patterns

By the mid-1970s it was becoming apparent that discrimination against women in computing existed and was being manifested in various ways. Employment data published by the US Department of Labour suggested that an increasing number of women were being employed in the manufacture of electronic computer equipment (Table 3).

	All employees	Women employees	Women as percentage
1967	145,100	39,700	27
1968	160,600	44,500	28
1969	182,700	50,400	28
1970	190,200	51,100	27
1971	170,100	43,600	25
1972	172,000	45,600	27
1973	189,900	55,700	29
1974	211,700	65,300	31

Table 3 US Employment — Electronic Computer Equipment

It is suggested (Weber and Gilchrist, 1975) that the indicated totals (Table 3) are too low. For example, one study (Gilchrist and Kapur, 1974) suggests that in 1973 the total employment by suppliers of computer equipment and related services was about 350,000. In any event the proportion of employed women at that time was probably about the 30 per cent suggested in the Department of Labour statistics.

Two of the principal ways in which discrimination manifests itself are in unequal access to higher-paid positions and in unequal pay for equal work. By the early 1970s, data was available to support charges that discrimination of these types existed in the US computer industry. 1970 census data (Table 4) suggests that fewer women, proportionately, tended to be employed as one ascended through the various skill (and status) levels of computer-user-related occupations.

Occupation	Male	Female	Total (000's)	% Female
Keypunch operator	27,896	244,674	272.6	89.7
Tab machine operator	4,118	4,042	8.2	49.5
Computer operator	83,023	34,199	117.2	29.2
Programmer	124,956	36,381	161.3	22.6
System analyst	68,213	11,736	79.3	14.7
Computer specialist	11,445	1,806	13.3	13.6
Dp repairman	30,844	864	31.7	2.7

Table 4   US Census Data (1970) for Computer User Related Occupations

That US women were not receiving equal pay for equal work in the computer industry of the early-1970s was shown by Area Wage Surveys (Table 5).

	Class A		Class B		Class C	
	%	Wage $	%	Wage $	%	Wage $
Keypunch operator						
Female	42	141	58	122	–	–
Male	53	178	47	136	–	–
Computer operator						
Female	12	192	55	157	33	137
Male	30	197	50	167	20	139
Business programmer						
Female	28	257	49	211	23	178
Male	38	265	47	221	15	186
Business systems analyst						
Female	26	313	53	266	21	222
Male	44	324	44	276	12	235

Table 5   Percentage at Skill Levels, and Mean Weekly Wage, for Computer User Occupations (US, 1973-1974)

Available figures for the US computer industry for the early 1970s show that at that time employed women did not have equality with men (and this despite the passing of the Equal Pay Act and Title VII of the 1964 Civil Rights Act, provisions intended to end employment and wage discrimination against women). It is possible to debate the reasons for this situation. Education was obviously relevant, as were possible age differences between men and women at various skill levels. However, it is likely that sexist attitudes within the industry contributed to effective discrimination.

In the mid-1970s there was growing concern about the degree of discrimination in the US computer industry. And, inevitably, extreme opinions were expressed: Judith Lightfoot, an officer of the National Organisation of Women, saw the overall picture of the industry 'as a disgrace' while one letter in a computer periodical declared: 'There is a much simpler solution to the problem of the underpaid female in DP: less brain, less pay.'

The journal *Computerworld*, sampling 30 women, found that eighteen of the group did not feel that they had been subjected to discrimination, though six thought that their companies were particularly good in this area and some of the women expected problems if they were to try to advance into management. Eighteen of the 30 women had been in the industry for more than four years, and nine of these reported discrimination. Only three of the twelve who had been in the industry for less than four years felt that they had been subject to discrimination. A survey of 327 women, reported in *Datamation* (August 1975), found that two-thirds of the respondents felt that they had broad equality with men in the industry.

However it is clear that women's perceptions in these areas may not accord with reality (see Table 5). Judith Lightfoot has suggested that women themselves sometimes believe misleading propaganda about the (relatively young) computer industry having avoided the traditional discrimination in other industries.

In another survey (Stone, 1977), 154 responses (88 women and 66 men) were analysed. To the first major question — 'Do you feel your organisation discriminates against women in the hiring, transfer, selection or promotion into DP positions?' — 56 respondents (42 women and 14 men) said yes, and 98 respondents (46 women and 52 men) said no. Thus 47 per cent of the women, but only 15 per cent of the men, thought that they detected discrimination against women.

The respondents came from installations of all sizes. In general, the larger installations seemed to trigger more feeling of discrimination than the smaller ones. And the percentage of women in an installation seemed to relate to the amount of perceived discrimination: on average, women were 35 per cent of the population of the centres thought to discriminate against women, but were 54 per cent of the population of those centres without evident bias. Again, care should be taken not to equate *perceived* discrimination with *actual* discrimination. In some cases (eg through the mechanism of scapegoating) discrimination may be only imagined. In many other instances, discrimination may operate in an organisation, but with male and female staff disposed to accept 'rationalisations' in terms of job suitability, differential aptitudes, or varying levels of experience.

We may expect the character of discrimination to vary from one country to another and from one data processing occupation to another. The 'shunting' of women into particular jobs only occurs with what are considered to be low-grade occupations. With higher-grade jobs male applicants may be deemed 'more suitable' than female, and women may have to demonstrate *superior* ability to men to be granted the *same* status. In some data processing occupations (eg programming), this situation is ironic.

Some observers point to the relatively high numbers of female programmers in the US to indicate the lack of discrimination in data processing. For women to constitute about 25 per cent of a particular profession may not seem all that impressive until one looks at the extent of their representation in the higher levels of professional activity. There are very few female dp managers and female executives of computer companies. And even the current numbers of female programmers have to be set against what was the situation in the early days of computing.

In one view (Kraft and Biggar, 1979), 'virtually 100% of the original programming workforce was comprised of women.' This refers to the women who programmed Eniac for the US War Department in 1944-46 at the Moore School of Electrical Engineering. The situation was that the Eniac engineers and scientists, mostly men, were concerned with designing and constructing the electronics hardware. It was assumed that the equipment's programming requirements were a mere clerical detail that could be dealt with at the appropriate time. In consequence, programming became for a short time one of the many clerical tasks automatically assigned to women – in this case to the 'Eniac girls', college graduates who had been appointed by the War Department to do manually what Eniac was supposed to do electronically.

The women were given a crash course in the machine's logic and other circuits, and were then expected to perform the 'clerical' task of designing and testing the Eniac programs. Some of the women were later sent to Los Alamos to program computers involved in the Manhattan Project, the design and development of the atomic bomb. They then returned to the job of programming Eniac to perform trajectory calculations, its original purpose.

After the war it was soon realised that programming was more than a mere clerical activity. (Kraft: 'Programming was therefore quickly redefined as creative and challenging work. It was also just as quickly redefined as men's work'.) Even the serious shortage of skilled computer specialists in the early 1950s and beyond did not encourage the emerging computer companies to employ, train and promote women on a basis of equality with men. Male employees were sought in preference to women, and the war-time accomplishments of female programmers were quickly forgotten ('Women programmers ... gradually dropped out of the field they had helped found').

The historical circumstances also give clues for an interpretation of the programming scene today. It is arguable, for example, that the seemingly high proportion of female programmers in the US computer industry is in fact misleading, that women were only allowed to advance in this sector when it became possible again to reduce certain types of programming work to 'mere clerical' activity. It is certainly true that most of the highly-skilled and best-paid jobs are held by men. This means that overall statistics on the number of women employed in any computer industry sector need to be interpreted with care.

In a paper read at the 1979 National Computer Conference, Helen M Wood of the National Bureau of Standards discussed available evidence on the position of women in the US data processing industry. Again it is emphasised that US government has supported equal opportunity for women and affirmative action (reference to the Civil Rights Act of 1964 and Executive Orders 10590 and 11375, prohibiting discrimination, on the basis of race, colour, religion, sex, national origin or age, in federal employment).

Evidence has been presented (eg by Weber and Gilchrist, 1975) to suggest 'that women are not receiving equal pay for equal work and may not be sharing equally in the opportunities for advancement'. There was also evidence adduced in the mid-1970s to suggest that the computer industry, despite discrimination, represented a relatively favourable employment environment for women. Reports produced by the National Science Foundation found, in 1974, that of the six per cent of all employed scientists and engineers who were women, the largest proportion (22 per cent) were classed as computer specialists.* It was found that 88 per cent of the female computer specialists in the scientist/engineer population were employed, compared to (eg) 53 per cent of the life scientists and 23 per cent of the total. This suggests better employment opportunities, at least in the mid-1970s, for female computer specialists than for female specialists in other technical disciplines. Again this says little about the character of the occupations concerned.

Helen Wood, at the 1979 NCC, concluded from the above and related data that, though women are disadvantaged in science and technology, some progress is being made. It is obvious that such progress is essential for the best use of national resources. The US National Science Foundation has pointed out that there is a clear under-utilisation of women in the sciences and engineering, both in terms of their access to these fields and their subsequent utilisation as members of the scientific workforce (1977 NSF report: 'there are relatively few women scientists, and even fewer engin-

* A term used to include college faculty posts in the computer sciences, computer programmers, computer systems analysts, computer scientists, etc.

eers').

In an address to the International Congress of Data Processing (Berlin, October 1980), Mrs Steve Shirley listed the broad discriminatory features of the computer industry:

— women are in the lower-paid job grades;

— they are at the lower end of each job grade;

— they spend longer in each job grade awaiting promotion;

— the proportion of women in each grade falls off very rapidly with increasing job grade.

Again it is worth emphasising that even where equal opportunities are backed by legislation, or declared company policy, women are at a considerable employment disadvantage. For example, in the UK, years after Equal Pay and Sex Discrimination laws have come into force, the average woman's wage is about 60 per cent of the average man's wage. And IBM and other large computer manufacturers, with declared policies on equal opportunities, employ very few women, proportionately, in senior technical or management positions.

The same points are emphasised by Robyn Dasey, research officer of the Association of Professsional, Executive, Clerical and Computer Staff and secretary of the union's Office Technology Committee. She points out that sexual discrimination is 'quite clear' (Dasey, 1980) — 'Women fill the lowest paid, monotonous, machine-paced jobs of the data preparation room. Men dominate the professional and managerial posts, whether as dp managers or systems analysts.' This observer sees the computing industry as 'in no way progressive' — 'in the suppliers' use of women in advertising literature and at sales exhibitions, it is second to none in the exploitation of women's appearance to sell its products'. Furthermore, Apex research confirms other work emphasising that women tend to be shunted into low-status jobs. A survey of UK staff in user companies showed that women constitute:

— 75-100 per cent of data preparation and data control staff;

— 10-25 per cent of operators;

— 5-15 per cent of programmers;

— less than 5 per cent of systems analysts.

In such circumstances it is hardly surprising that there is a short-age of skilled staff in the computer industry. There is an obvious reservoir of (female) potential that (predominantly male) manage-ments seem reluctant to develop.

What is evident in the US and the UK is also true of other devel-oped countries. Reporters from the German magazine *Computer-woche* have noted that German women are less than happy about their employment chances in the computer industry. An interview was conducted with 50 women programmers, systems analysts and data processing managers (reported by John Lamb, 1980). It was found that women had lower positions and promotion prospects than men employed in the same work.

It was felt that women had to start lower in the company hier-archy, that different standards were applied to the performance of men and women ('when a woman makes a mistake, the comment is, "she's only a woman". If a man makes it, then it's "nobody is perfect". There is a difference'), and that various difficulties arose simply because a person was a woman. Again there is evidence of 'shunting' and of discriminatory pay policies. Kienbaum Consult-ants produced figures in 1979 indicating that 96.9 per cent of German data preparation staff are women, with female systems analysts, programmers and sales staff accounting for only 18 per cent of the total (12,927 women out of 97,260 professional dp staff).

The same research organisation also established that in a list of 23 different types of job — ranging from head of management services down to data preparation operator — women are almost always paid less than men. A male keyboard operator in Germany will earn about £400 more, on average, than a woman doing the same work. A male dp manager will earn around £6000 a year more than a female dp manager. Only among systems analysts were women found to have a salary advantage (men on average earn £12,700 a year, women just under £13,500*). In some job categories, women were so rare that they are not mentioned in survey data. (A *Computerwoche* interviewee observed that 'men

* Figures for 1979 survey by Kienbaum Consultants.

just won't consider women in the same light as their fellow men when it comes to promotion to more important, meaningful posts'.)

Figures for Norway for 1975, provided by Kirsti Berg, chairwoman of a Norwegian data processing consultant company, show the predictable pattern of female representation in the various data processing job categories:

− key punching and computer operation − 50 per cent;

− system analysis, design and programming − 14 per cent;

− management and sales − 9 per cent.

As we have seen, the reasons for this situation lie partly in the industry and partly in the way women are influenced by education and other cultural factors to take up one career or another. In 1978, about a half of all students entering graduate studies in Norway were women. The percentage choosing economics, for example, was around sixteen, whereas only 8 per cent chose engineering. Berg suggests that women are discouraged from developing an interest in technical studies. One Norwegian study found that girls were artificially graded low in mathematics while boys were artificially graded high − to create the right framework of incentives and disincentives!

Activities within the Norwegian data processing industry also have women under-represented, even bearing in mind how their numbers grow smaller as one ascends the 'status ladder' of dp occupations. For example, female participation at major conferences is only a half of what would be expected according to the percentage of women in the business. And with regard to membership of the Norwegian Computer Society, the number of women listed as 'company representatives' is only a third of what may be expected. Evidently for domestic, company or other reasons, women are discouraged from attending conferences and other meetings that are likely to develop their careers.

Kirsti Berg envisages a deterioration in the position of women vis-a-vis the computer industry in the years to come − 'Strong means have to be applied if the trend is to be turned.'

A survey of UK Dataskil staff, reported by Pamela Poe of Key Communications, revealed some of the perceived barriers to female advancement in the computer industry.* Thirty-three of the 70 Dataskil women were asked about previous jobs and how they came to be employed by Dataskil. The women are technicians, project leaders and managers, systems analysts, programmers and consultants. One conclusion was that 'traditional approaches to career counselling have, in the past, contributed to women not even considering a career in DP'.

In another poll, 21 women were encouraged to talk about perceived sexual discrimination. With one exception they felt they had not encountered job or promotion-related sexual discrimination in Dataskil. One view was that women should strive to break out of the traditional female occupations and then 'prove themselves'. Again there is awareness of the difficulties that women face in trying to develop a dp career. A paper from the 1978 National Computer Conference is quoted: 'Computer science education and immediate employment on the first steps of the career ladder are readily available for women but after these initial steps women still face cultural, educational, and institutional barriers which block them from advancement to the top.'

Data accumulated by the National Computing Centre suggests that 'women may well form an untapped reservoir of potential computer staff — and certainly more should be done to attract back, perhaps on a part-time basis, women who left the industry to start families' (Simpson, 1979). It is worth comparing male and female data derived from the sample. The number of men and women in particular dp occupations is significant (Table 6). It is clear that this data provides no support for the popular prejudice that women change jobs more frequently than men do.

The data suggests that women have to be better qualified than men to be acceptable in the same job. Thus female programmers are much more likely to be graduates than are male programmers, and this difference cannot be explained by the fact that some men are older: whatever the age, female programmers tend to be better academically qualified than male programmers. This is also true for systems analysts but less evident in other dp occupations.

* See also Appendix 1.

FEMALE Job Title	Number	Years in Job			Age		
		Min	Av	Max	Min	Av	Max
DP Manager	0	—	—	—	—	—	—
Systems Manager/Chief	3	1	2.6	4	27	33	37
Programming Manager/Chief	5	1	2.5	4	25	29.6	37
Operations Manager/Chief	4	0	3.7	10	25	33.3	43
Systems Analyst	18	0	2.9	7	22	26.9	34
Analyst/Designer	8	0	1.7	4	22	27.8	44
Analyst/Programmer	25	0	2.3	6	23	26.9	38
Programmer	59	0	2.9	9	19	24.5	38
Systems Programmer	3	0	1.1	2	24	27.3	29
Computer Operator	39	0	3.8	8	18	24.2	39
MALE							
DP Manager	22	0	3.8	14	27	39.9	56
Systems Manager/Chief	61	0	2.9	10	27	36.4	54
Programming Manager/Chief	41	0	3.1	15	26	34.4	54
Operations Manager/Chief	53	0	3.3	11	23	33.6	55
Systems Analyst	156	0	3.7	15	22	31.3	51
Analyst/Designer	59	0	2.9	10	21	31.9	52
Analyst/Programmer	76	0	2	10	18	28.4	51
Programmer	154	0	3.3	20	19	26.6	57
Systems Programmer	25	0	2.2	6	22	28.4	37
Computer Operator	123	0	3.9	10	17	24.6	49

Table 6   Ages and Years in Job for DP Job Categories (Source: Simpson, 1979)

It is also worth asking why more experienced and qualified women do not return to computing after leaving to start a family. Women in this position represent an evident pool of valuable labour. It has been suggested that people may be worried about coping, after a lengthy absence, in a fast-moving technical industry (Simpson: 'From limited personal interviews and correspondence it seems to me that such women have read about micros and data bases, etc, and think that they have been left far behind by technology'). Such worries are at least partly misplaced, and there is a clear obligation on managements to provide the necessary training.*

It has long been apparent that a valuable pool of female labour was available and could be exploited by the computer industry. In 1973, Suzette Harold of F International could observe that a supply of suitable female labour in the professional range coexisted with a shortage of suitable male labour. And in February 1980 the UK Department of Industry noted that the 13,000 female workers in the computer manufacturing industry accounted for only about 27 per cent of the total workforce. And this is despite a figure of around 40 per cent women employed in the national economy as a whole.

We have seen that in circumstances of economic recession women's jobs are under greater threat than those of men, and that today there are no grounds for complacency regarding the position of women in employment. At the same time there are success stories which should be taken as encouraging. For example, Christine Harvey (*Computer Weekly*, 8/6/78) describes the career circumstances of a number of successful women in the data pro-cessing industry (see also the examples in Chapters 1, 3 and 5).

Faye Ogilvie, director of Management and Executive Selection, placed a woman in the computer sales field several years ago — with great success ('This woman was so successful that her com-pany hired a chauffeur-driven car for her to see her clients'). In another case a woman had been placed with a company, and after three years the boss rang Ogilvie: 'Can you help me fill her spot with another woman? She's moving abroad with her husband, and she's done such a tremendous job, I don't think her clients will accept a man in her place. I want to fill it with another woman.'

The National Computing Centre has seen significant progress in the position of women in its own sales staff. Today, from a situa-tion ten years ago in which there were virtually no women in sales there are now six female regional-office staff out of a total of 22. The women, on average slightly younger than the men, are graded the same. One of the female regional officers was formerly an NCC secretary, a circumstance that illustrates the enhanced opportuni-

* The 1980/81 UK economic recession did not help: see 'British Firms Skip Training', *Electronics Weekly*, 31/12/80–7/1/81, p 1

ties for secretaries in this organisation. (In NCC, thirteen ex-secretaries are now in administrative posts.)

However, there can be disadvantages in being a woman in sales. Kay Law, the first woman in sales in the Page Printing Systems Division at Honeywell, is quoted by Harvey: 'While my colleagues accuse me of having prejudice working in my favour, I argue that it also creates a time-wasting factor. Because women in this field are such a rarity, men sometimes make appointments just to see what a saleswoman is like, with no intention of buying.' The women interviewed by Harvey implied that they were not 'women's libbers', but often believed that being female had helped their careers (Sonya Howell Jones: 'If you have sound reasoning and good judgement, you can use your charm as the final straw').

Christine Stott, sales promotion manager for Case, has declared that 'one is very conscious of the fact that men have constraints towards working for a woman which is a source of concern.' And she readily acknowledges the problems that women face in seeking to develop a career in the data processing industry – 'First, it takes women longer to establish credibility. Second, they must always be prepared to walk the tightrope between femininity and professionalism. Also, they must take the same attitude towards work as men do, including working late and taking business luncheons for granted' (quoted by Harvey).

Summary

The successes of particular women in data processing do not, as we have seen, indicate a situation of equal opportunities in the industry. It is convenient to list some of the problems indicated in the present section:

- Girls are discouraged from taking an interest in technical matters. Instead they are channelled into areas 'appropriate to their sex';

- In schools and colleges, girls are discouraged from opting for scientific and technical courses (see below);

- Employers have different job expectations of women. This leads to the shunting of women into low-grade work, inadequate training facilities for women, and pay discrimination policies that work against women;

— Women often have to be better qualified than men to achieve
the same employment level. 'They have attained such positions by being undeniably far more qualified for them than
any of the men who might represent alternate choices' (Walsh,
1977);

— Double standards often attach to the evaluation of male and
female performance in employment. A woman's mistakes will
tend to underwrite stereotyping ('She's only a woman'). A
man's mistakes will not be interpreted in sexual terms ('We're
all human');

— There are 'nebulous' problems faced by women, eg male condescension and the subtle exclusion of women from male
'networking' patterns.

Compared with other, older industries, it is arguable that
women have done well in data processing. But this case has to be
evaluated with care. There is massive exploitation of cheap female
labour in South-East Asia and elsewhere for the fabrication of
electronic components. And traditional discriminatory pressures
are working to shunt women into relatively low-grade jobs in data
processing in the developed world (eg data preparation tasks,
formalised commercial programming, etc). In the computer industry, as elsewhere, it is not difficult to find evidence of a complex
of discriminatory attitudes and practices that work to the disadvantage of women.

EDUCATION

It is apparent that discriminatory pressures exert an influence on
women long before they become employed in the data processing,
or any other, industry. Some feminists would like us to consider
how the handling of babies in their first days, or even hours, of life
helps to lay the basis of the stereotyping that is developed in childhood and adolescence, and consolidated in adult life. But for our
purposes we do not need to start so early. However, we should
consider education, — which, so far, has been mentioned but not
discussed in any detail.

There is increasing evidence that girls begin schooling less equipped than boys to develop technical interests. There *may* be a 'nature' element that contributes to this situation (I cannot be completely insensitive to the work of Corinne Hutt and other like-minded researchers), but it is clear that boys are encouraged to develop technical interests in ways that girls are not. This seems to be evident in the early years at school and later, when there is real scope for technical education.

In November 1980 a report, *Girls and Science*, was published by the Department of Education and Science. This followed an investigation by HM inspectors who visited fifteen comprehensive schools where the proportion of girls studying science was higher than the national average. One conclusion was that pupils in girls-only schools are more likely to enjoy science than are girls in mixed schools, where they are discouraged by having to compete with boys. (This conclusion accords with the results* obtained from 10,000 questionnaires completed by fourth-formers in secondary schools.)

It was found that even in schools with a relatively high proportion of girls studying science, the girls worry about appearing stupid in front of the boys. There was evidence that girls see boys as 'cleverer', even when there was no information to suggest such an impression. Girls tend to lack confidence in approaching practical work because they have had less previous practical experience than boys in such practical jobs as mending fuses and repairing bicycles.

The inspectors also found that the physical sciences were seen as 'boys' subjects' − not only by the girls themselves, but also by some parents and teachers. (Educational and psychological research has shown how 'expectations' can influence performance, even among young people of equal ability.) It was suggested that girls be given more science in primary schools to prepare them better for secondary education. Girls in the HMI survey were reluctant to become involved in class discussions for fear of giving

* Published, as the report *Teenage Attitudes to Technology and Industry* (by Ray Page and Melanie Nash of Bath University), by the Standing Conference on Schools Science and Technology.

wrong answers in front of the boys. It is obvious that a preparation for technical confidence and competence in girls must begin
as early as possible.

Catherine Avent, a careers guidance inspector for the ILEA and
a member of the Finniston Committee, sees a place for compul-
sion in the preparation of girls for technical careers. For example,
there should be compulsory mathematics to O Level standard: 'I
don't believe that any girl should be allowed to drop any maths
subject just because she is not interested in it. I know of no boys
who are allowed to drop it.' Furthermore, 'Most girls who have the
capacity to become technicians are keeping up maths, but only
71% are offered the choice of physics ... only 5% of the total number of girls pass. So the majority never have the opportunity to
become engineers' (quoted in *The Engineer*, 10/4/80). And there
is the familiar observation that women may offer *more* than men,
once women do make the grade: 'once a company has employed
a female engineer, it takes on lots more' (*The Engineer*).

By the time women reach higher education they are relatively
disinclined to pursue a technical career. Thirty-six per cent of
university under-graduates in the UK are women, but only twelve
per cent of physics students are female and the representation of
women in engineering and technology is less than four per cent. It
is suggested (Barton et al, 1980) that 'the position of women is
unlikely to change significantly.' The proportion of females taking
apprenticeships in engineering and related industries has scarcely
changed over the last decade (Table 7).

	TOTALS		AS % OF ALL EMPLOYEES	
	Male	Female	Male	Female
1970	150,260	950	5.4	0.1
1971	144,000	1030	5.3	0.1
1972	128,110	770	4.9	0.1
1973	105,390	440	4.3	0.1
1974	94,070	580	3.8	0.1
1975	97,080	970	3.8	0.1
1976	95,300	990	4.0	0.1
1977	100,420	980	4.2	0.1
1978	106,110	1310	4.4	0.2

Table 7   UK Apprentices in Engineering and Related Industries
(Source: Department of Employment Gazette)

A survey of 93 companies (33 in engineering, 29 in textiles, 10 in chemicals and 21 in other manufacturing sectors) showed an overwhelming male dominance in technically skilled jobs (Table 8). The number of firms increasing their number of technically qualified women was low.

	Male	Female
HNC/D in technical subjects	984	48
Degree in technical subjects	558	48
Postgraduates in technical subjects	78	1
Apprenticeships completed	4731	13
Professional qualifications	1261	35
On internal technical courses	128	50
On day-release technical courses	1257	162
On external technical courses	177	9

**Table 8 Qualifications of Employees in Sample Firms
(Source: Barton et al, 1980)**

When asked about the prospects for the training and employment of technically qualified women in their industry, more than a quarter of the sample firms anticipated improvement over the next five years; and less than a third thought that the prospects would not improve. More than 40 per cent answered 'can't say' to this question.

The main reason why firms were not recruiting technically-qualified women was that they simply were not available. One small firm declared that *no* females applied for craft apprenticeships. Another company referred to the 'low level of response of females to advertisements'. A large chemical firm observed that 'the ratio of female graduates to male is small.' Again it is possible to trace the difficulty to the schools, where early attitudes are formed.

In March 1978 the Engineering Industry Training Board (EITB) announced a three-point plan supporting positive discrimination in favour of women in the area of training:

- Up to 250 grants of £5000 awarded to firms recruiting extra girls to train as technicians or engineers;

- 50 undergraduate bursaries of £1500 each for women reading engineering in a degree course approved by the Council of Engineering Institutions and of 'major interest' to manufacturing industry;

- 'Insight 1979', a one-week residential course to help sixth-form girls studying mathematics and science to learn about careers in engineering.

Some suggestions are set in the context of only one engineer in 500 in the UK being a woman, compared with one in 50 in the US, and one in three in the USSR. (The EITB plan is described in detail in *Industrial and Commercial Training*, December 1979.)

Some awards are designed to encourage females in engineering. For example, in 1980 Fenella Hume, a project leader at Kent Industrial Measurements, was named Girl Technician Engineer of the Year, an award sponsored by the IEETE and the Caroline Haslett Memorial Trust. Hume received £250 and an inscribed rose bowl.

The situation in data processing education reflects that in the broader field of science and technology. There are comparatively fewer women undertaking computer courses. Figures from the Universities Central Council on Admissions (UCCA) show the relatively poor representation of women in these areas. For example, the total number of applicants for computer science courses for October 1978 was 2336 (1677 men and 659 women), with registrations totalling 1397 (1014 men and 383 women). In October 1979 there were 3267 applicants (2380 men and 887 women). Again the suggestion is that the figures are a reflection of how girls are channelled during their early school education. Similar patterns emerge for the computer courses run by particular educational institutions, eg Thames Polytechnic (Table 9).

The Threshold Scheme, run by the National Computing Centre and supported by Government grant, is designed to give training and job experience in operating and programming. The course lasts 40 weeks (16 of which are spent at college and 24 in industry), and applicants need not have academic qualifications.

	B.Sc Maths		HND Maths Stats & Computing		HND Computer Studies		B.Sc. Computer Science	
	Male	Female	Male	Female	Male	Female	Male	Female
1974-1975	53	18	23	6	39	9	15	3
1975-1976	38	15	29	7	31	5	34	7
1976-1977	35	13	28	4	39	7	51	13
1977-1978	42	14	34	7	51	16	72	20
1978-1979	38	19	34	6	55	13	88	20
1979-1980	59	25	37	14	54	22	93	29

Table 9   Student Numbers for Thames Polytechnic Mathematics and Computer Courses (1974-1980)

George Penney, of NCC, has said that the ratio of applicants was five male to four female.

The aptitude tests used in the selection of applicants comprise a) general reasoning, b) spatial ability, c) clerical ability and accuracy and d) observation and clear thinking. It has been found that the boys are marginally better in a), b) and d), with the girls significantly better in c). The ratio of successful applicants to the Threshold scheme is three male to two female.

In the US, women appear to have made little progress, in terms of computer course enrolment and graduation, over the last decade. In one study (reported by Montanelli and Mamrak, 1976) for the first half of the 1970s, it was found that except at the bachelor's level there had been no increase in the percentage of women enrolled in, or graduated from, computer science degree programmes. It was also found that there was a decrease in the percentage of women enrolled in, or graduated from, computer science degree courses as the level of the degree rose (ie women received 18 per cent of bachelor's degrees, 15 per cent of master's degrees, and 7 per cent of the doctorates). It was obvious that women were neither enrolling in, nor graduating from, computer science degree courses in proportion to their representation in the population as a whole.

The mid-1970s showed some promising signs for the progress of women in computer faculties. For example, a study in late-1975 (reported by Mamrak and Monanelli, 1978) showed broad equality between men and women as faculty members. And, in terms of faculty graduations, the 1970s can be seen as better than the 1960s. During the seventies women gained more than 20 per cent of bachelor's degrees in computer science (compared with 12.5 per cent during the sixties). By 1978, women were receiving 25.8 per cent of the bachelor's degrees and 18.7 per cent of the master's degrees. At the same time it is clear that progress is slow (Figures 2, 3 and 4).

A study completed by the Evaluation and Training Institute for the National Science Foundation (reported by Rose and Bolus, 1980) focussed on the enrolment and academic employment patterns of women scientists and engineers in eight science and mathematics fields, including computer science. The study detected that an increasing number of women were receiving graduate training in these fields, but noted that many women entering the academic job market are receiving low-status, low-salary research positions rather than the higher-status, better-paid faculty positions. There was also evidence of companies trying to attract women computer science graduates by offering high salaries and strong career possibilities.

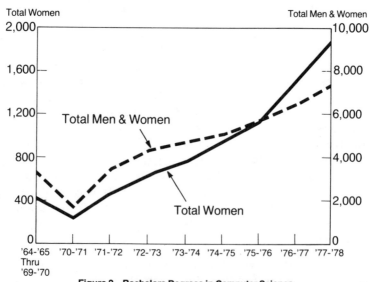

Figure 2   Bachelors Degrees in Computer Science

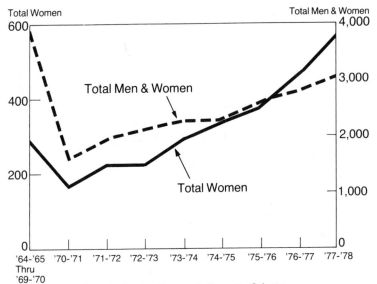

Figure 3   Masters Degrees in Computer Science

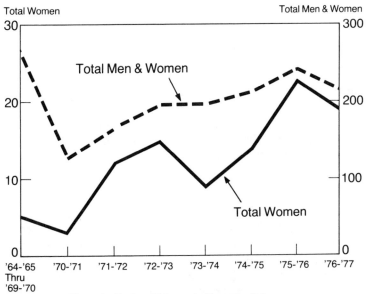

Figure 4   Doctoral Degrees in Computer Science

Some US programmes are developed specifically to help women transfer from one academic technical area to another. For example, in 1980 the University of Texas was awarded $132,420 from the National Science Foundation to conduct a project for women wanting to transfer from poor opportunity technical fields to computer science. The project provides self-paced retraining courses and is intended to become part of the university's regular educational programme. Under the NSF scheme, funds will be provided for the university to recruit and train women in computer science during the 1981-1983 period (*Computerworld*, 28/7/80). The NSF has presented 23 awards, totalling $1,021,011, with the intention of increasing the number of women in scientific and technical fields. The annual awards, made under NSF's Women in Science programme, will support 17 science career workshops and six science career facilitation projects in the US.

In September 1980, Women in Data-Processing (WDP) announced a series of technical and personal development seminars. The organisation is to offer assertiveness training, specially designed for women in the computer field. Sessions on 'networking for women' have been held and more are planned. Such schemes aim to develop the confidence of women in the computer industry and to overcome the traditional barriers to their advancement.

It is clear that in the field of education there is no room for complacency. Women are relatively poorly represented – in the UK, the US and elsewhere – as applicants to computer courses, as graduates, and as senior faculty members. There is growing consciousness of steps that need to be taken to increase the number of women taking computer subjects in institutions of higher education. It remains to be seen whether this consciousness will be translated into effective action.

SUMMARY

There is a new awareness of the needs of women in employment in general and in the computer industry in particular. However there is still evidence of stereotyping and discriminatory practices and attitudes at many levels of education and employment. The new consciousness of discrimination against women has yielded impressive (but often incomplete) legislation in many countries, but this has had less impact for equal opportunities, equal pay, etc, than many people hoped.

Discriminatory pressures begin in schools and are (more or less) consistently maintained throughout the early years of education. In such circumstances it is hardly surprising that there are relatively few female applicants for computer science courses at universities and polytechnics, and relatively few female applicants for high-powered computer jobs in industry, commerce, government and education. Again it is clear that the position of women in the data processing industry cannot be divorced from discriminatory attitudes in the other areas of the broader culture.

3 Women in Management

INTRODUCTION

The position of women with regard to management highlights how far they have to travel before a situation of equal opportunities is a reality. Just as women tend to be shunted into low-grade jobs, so they are prevented — by a complex of social mechanisms — from appearing, in any significant numbers, in management ranks. Female supervisors in such areas as retailing and manufacturing are more common than female line managers or female senior managers: this also is highly significant — female management skills are most likely to be acknowledged and encouraged in job sectors that are already predominantly staffed by women, ie in relatively low-grade occupations.

In any branch of industry or commerce, female directors and managers are heavily outnumbered by their male counterparts. By the late-1970s the Institute of Directors had 800 women members, 3.5 per cent of the 27,000 total, and the British Institute of Management had 704 women members, only 1.23 per cent of the 57,387 total. The female proportion of senior staff is low for all sectors of the economy, and appears not to be changing. Today, with more than 40 per cent of the total UK workforce women, only about 2 per cent of professionals, employers and managers are women. In most technical institutes women constitute an even lower proportion of the membership. For example, women comprise a mere 0.2 per cent of the membership of the Institution of Mechanical Engineers. The pattern varies over the various institutes but in all instances women are a small minority of total membership (figures for 1978):

83

Institute of Bankers — 12 per cent

Institute of Chartered Accountants — 2.8 per cent

Institution of Civil Engineers — 0.15 per cent

Institute of Supervisory Management — 2.0 per cent

The Law Society — 7.0 per cent

In education, a profession that has traditionally encouraged women, it is significant that whereas 74 per cent of primary school teachers and 43 per cent of secondary school teachers are women, only 25 per cent of heads and deputies are women. Similarly in law, 8 per cent of barristers and 2.3 per cent of judges are women. In technical industries, as we would expect, there are relatively few female managers: in the chemical industry, for example, where 50 per cent of the total workforce are women, only 5 per cent of managers are women. The above figures are for the UK. It is interesting to look also at the female percentage of administrators and managers for other countries (Table 10).

Country	Year	Percentage
Finland	1976	14.4
Italy	1971	5.7
Netherlands	1971	4.4
Norway	1977	13.2
Sweden	1977	9.0
USA	1977	22.2

Table 10   Women as Percentage of Administrators and Managers (Source: 1978 Year Book of Statistics)

It is clear that the representation of women at senior levels is low in all professions. Less than a fifth of all doctors in hospitals are female, and around one tenth of consultants. In the Civil Service little more than a tenth of the higher administrative posts are held by women, and only 4 per cent of Assistant Secretaries are women. The poor representation of women in senior posts is a worldwide phenomenon. Even in Eastern Europe, where large numbers of women qualify as technicians, they rarely reach the higher levels of management. For example, in the USSR only 6 per cent of directors of industrial enterprises are female. (This circumstance suggests that there are powerful forces, apart from educational disadvantage, working against the advancement of women.)

At the same time, there *are* successful women supervisors, administrators and managers (see Profiles ..., below). And particular companies are keen to foster progressive attitudes with respect to equal opportunities. For example, CMG Computer Management Group (Scotland), which won the Confederation of British Industry's 1980 Award for Employee Involvement, is prepared to encourage the movement of women up to the management ranks. A former secretary, who only joined the company after her children had grown up, is now a CMG director. But the existence of a few progressive companies scarcely shows that all is well. There are practical measures that can be taken, in the UK and elsewhere, to further the advancement of women in the computer industry and in other areas of economic activity (see Steps ..., below).

DISCRIMINATION

The relatively small number of women in data processing management suggests the existence of discriminatory pressures. However, some successful female dp managers state that they have felt no discrimination. Dr Marion Wood, an Assistant Professor at the University of Southern California, with responsibilities for training women for management, has pointed out that data processing is not historically a male-dominated profession (as are such occupations as dentistry, law and engineering). Data processing is represented as having little or no 'access discrimination' (where women are not encouraged to enter the field), as always having been open to both men and women. But again a distinction needs to be made between the *perception* of discrimination and its *existence*. Successful women can be oblivious to real discriminatory forces. In one study (Levitin et al, 1971), a national survey of 539 American working women revealed that only 7.9 per cent of them were aware of *any* discrimination, whereas there was objective evidence of discrimination against 95 per cent of these women.

There are various reasons for the apparent gap between 'perception' and 'reality'. Women may have a psychological vested interest in making the best of a bad situation. They may themselves have discriminatory attitudes which work against their own career development. And they may only think of *overt* discrimination, neglecting less obvious discriminatory factors.

It is hard to avoid the conclusion that discrimination acts in many ways to restrict the advancement of women in data processing and other professions (see also Chapter 2). A detailed mid-1970s survey (*EDP Analyzer*, August 1976) concluded that though 'there appears to be little salary discrimination against women in the computer field, we conclude that there *is* systematic discrimination' (original italics). That there are few women at the higher levels of the computing industry was based 'on company personnel procedures as well as cultural attitudes'. It is likely that the situation in data processing has not changed much since that time.

One survey, reported in *Computerworld* (Dooley, 1979), found that male data processing employees can expect to be promoted to management almost three years earlier than their female colleagues. The women respondents claimed that men who were appointed to the same position and at the same time worked an average of 5.5 years before becoming managers while the women had to work 8.4 years before gaining similar promotion. In one company it was observed that only men were hired as managers, and one woman observed that the man who started with her is now her immediate superior. Most of the women surveyed believed that discrimination was a real problem for women in data processing, but that this was less so once women became managers.

The situation was graphically highlighted by the difficulty in finding women managers to interview for the survey. One directory, containing the names of several thousand computer executives, carried the names of fewer than 10 female managers. Eventually *Computerworld* interviewed 25 women — who held various titles ranging from senior project leader to senior vice-president. Forty per cent of the women claimed that they had been denied promotion, at some point in their career, because of their sex, and 16 per cent said that they did not know whether discrimination had affected their progress.

Most of the women believed that there are double standards in hiring men and women, 64 per cent believing that women are judged differently to men when they are considered for posts in data processing. Again there is the common impression that women have to be better than men to be treated equally. In addition, women are obliged to overcome stereotypes, to compensate for 'being women', and to fit in with the requirements of male executives. No less than 28 per cent had at some time left a job because of discriminatory practices, and one woman had stayed where she was because 'it wasn't any better anywhere else.'

Some of the women also recognised that they had to fight discrimination before entering data processing. 36 per cent claimed that they had been actively discouraged from pursuing science or mathematics at school, whereas 24 per cent said that they had been encouraged to follow such subjects. Once the women entered the dp industry they experienced the same patterns of discrimination that exist in other, more traditional, industries; but 76 per cent of the respondents reckoned that the computer industry was better than other fields for opportunities for women (some suggested that this was only so because of a shortage of staff).

Thirty-six per cent of the women reported that, as managers, they had experienced work-related problems because of their sex. Some suggested that female employees found it more difficult to work for a woman than for the stereotypical male supervisor. About half the respondents claimed that their companies made no conscious effort to recruit women for management and executive positions. It was suggested that some companies deliberately restricted the recruitment of women to senior positions for 'fear of having too many women managers'.

The situation revealed in this survey is a familiar one. Women are discouraged from pursuing a technical career. When they persist and eventually enter the data processing industry, recruitment policies tend to be biased against them and, when they are appointed, their advancement within the organisation is often artificially delayed. There are signs that computing is less hide-bound than older traditional industries, but there is evidence also that women may not be aware of some of the powerful discriminatory pressures in the working environment.

ATTITUDES TO FEMALE MANAGERS

The advancement of women within an organisation can be affected by prevailing attitudes in established company policy, in male
colleagues, and in subordinates. Women themselves may be influenced by a complex of influential attitudes that lack real support
in fact (see also Female Characteristics, below).

Company attitudes are obviously crucial to female advancement.
One observer (Crisp, 1978) has pointed out how women can be
restricted in developing a banking career. Anyone hoping for
career progression within the bank in question is required to take
the examinations of the Institute of Bankers. However, whereas
men are encouraged to take the exams, it is 'assumed' that women
will not. A consequence is that the vast majority of women remain
in the clerical grades (out of the bank's 2983 managers, only 20
are women). The women who *do* persist in their career efforts
have more drive, on average, than their male colleagues.

The bulk of female managers in the bank are over 40 and single.
Once it is clear that a woman is unlikely to marry, it appears that
the company is prepared to consider her as a career possibility. As
with the survey of female dp managers cited in the above section,
the promotion of women is delayed for reasons that have nothing
to do with merit. (Crisp: 'Women as managers are generally seen
by their companies to be very conscientious and their diligence is
perceived as their great stength.')

The paucity of female executives is, as may be expected, an
international phenomenon. For example, a study by Kienbaum
Unternehmensberatung in Gummersbach (near Cologne) showed
that only 0.9 per cent of the 680 top German executives taking
part in the survey were women. And again it is possible to argue
that this situation is one largely conditioned by prevailing male
attitudes.

A study by Carl H Liebrecht Personnel Consultants tried to
ascertain the attitudes of male managers to their female counterparts (reported by Delamaide, 1979). A majority of male managers,
particularly those in younger-age and lower-salary brackets, were

in favour in principle of women executives, but are less sure when the question becomes more concrete. They 'are still governed largely by traditional role concepts in judging what qualities make a woman executive desirable (or undesirable) and which industries or positions are most suited to women managers'. And where women do advance to a management position, they are likely to be paid less than men. The Kienbaum study found that women managers in general receive salaries that are 20 per cent below those of their male counterparts — 'This difference is primarily based on sex.'

There is evidence that many organisations, in the UK and elsewhere, see 'the married male manager as an asset and the married female manager as a liability' (Davidson and Cooper, 1980). Prejudice against married female managers can exert pressure on aspiring women to remain single or to remain childless, options that no *male* manager would be expected to consider.

Attitudes of subordinates are also important to the advancement of women to the management ranks. If a woman is supervising a recalcitrant and uncooperative department, there may be reluctance to promote further. In fact, studies indicate that staff tend to view their female supervisors in a broadly 'positive' way. The US Department of Labour study (1978), examining the position of women in traditionally male jobs, investigated the extent of prejudice against female supervisors. Interviews were carried out with 56 subordinates (23 female and 33 male) of women in formerly-male managerial or supervisory positions. An early question in each interview was how the person felt about having a female boss in what had always been a male job. The results are given in Table 11.

When questions were asked about the performance of female supervisors the results indicated general satisfaction. There were signs that a woman has to perform better than a male counterpart in order to be rated 'good' or 'excellent'. A common belief was that female supervisors worked harder than did most male supervisors. It has also been stated that 'the more competent a woman is, the less difficult it is for men to work with and for her' (Barton, quoted by Snyders and Miles, 1980).

	Men	Women
Very negative	2	0
Generally negative	4	2
Mixed feelings	8	3
Generally positive	18	12
Very positive	1	6

Table 11   Attitudes to Female Supervisors
(Source: R & D Monograph 65, US Department of Labour)

The data processing industry cannot be considered in isolation from the mainstream ideas and attitudes of the broader culture. Successful dp women will encounter condescension and hostility from some men (and women) working in the same environment (see, for example, Walsh, 1977 and Sanders, 1978). Many female dp managers and executives, vigorous and robust as they have had to be, will ignore such attitudes. However, prevailing prejudice can be highly discouraging to young women contemplating a career in computing. It is in the interest of companies to take measures to enlarge the career possibilities open to women.

CURRENT PLANS TO ADVANCE WOMEN

Most companies, in data processing and other industry sectors, do not see an equal-opportunities problem. In fact they sometimes argue that to analyse or monitor the women's situation in their own organisation is itself discriminatory. (More than one organisation that the author approached for information argued in such a way.) The argument is superficially attractive — surely people should be treated equally, irrespective of sex! However, this approach is less attractive when it is realised that various discriminatory pressures are always present in most organisations (we have already looked at the character of some of these pressures). In such an environment an equal-opportunities programme that takes specific account of the disadvantaged position of women may be the only sensible approach. We may conclude that it is insufficient — and uneconomic — for companies in the UK and elsewhere to pretend that there is no problem.

Some organisations have introduced specific equal-opportunities schemes (see discussion of Rank Xerox, Chapter 2). Some US companies have been driven to introduce such programmes in the wake of large court-ordered settlements against firms that thought they were complying with existing laws. Cases in the UK, following the equal-pay and sex-discrimination legislation, have been less dramatic (see the Index to Cases, Wainwright, 1979, pp 283-289, for a listing of minorities' and women's cases).

In 1972, the personnel and employee development department of Southern California Edison reviewed its personnel system to assess its effectiveness in the light of the federal equal-opportunity laws. The company, a major electric utility with headquarters just east of Los Angeles, has 13,000 employees, 300 of whom are in the data processing division. SCE serves 2.8 million customers in the Southern California area, and has annual operating revenues of more than $1.7 billion.

After studying its personnel system, SCE decided that the equal employment awareness programme and the management training programmes being obtained from outside sources could be done better and more economically by its own personnel. The company developed a series of programmes, beginning with an affirmative action awareness programme which, since 1972, has been presented to all employees. Emphasis is given to SCE's objective of offering equal opportunities to all, irrespective of race or sex. Ability and performance are the crucial factors, and women and minorities are encouraged to compete with others on an equal basis.

It is a policy of SCE to promote from within for all company positions, unless no suitably-qualified in-house staff can be found. SCE sees this practice as a major way in which more women (and people from racial minorities) will be placed in the higher positions of the company. As many as 25,000 people apply for jobs with SCE every year, but most of these applicants are white males. In order to increase the likelihood of hiring minorities and women, the company takes active steps to recruit through women's organisations, through advertising in publications read by racial minorities and by women, and by using selected personnel agencies.

A professional appraisal form has been developed to discover which employees have the ability and willingness to progress to higher levels in the company. At least once a year, managers fill out the forms for subordinates stating whether the person is ready for promotion, what work the person is best at, what further training is necessary, etc. Training programmes have been developed for staff at different levels. The first-level course, aimed as a 'consciousness-raising' programme, was originally designed only for women, but it was found that men also could derive benefits from it.

It has often been emphasised (eg in *EDP Analyzer*, August 1976) that a key factor in moving women into management is a 'positive corporate environment'. SCE, with this in mind, has introduced various positive corporate policies – positive recruitment, internal promotions, appraisals, awareness programmes, training, etc. At the same time it has to be acknowledged that highly competent women might not be willing to accept promotion. SCE has found a number of women in this category. There may be reluctance to work for further qualifications, to accept overtime demands, or to embrace the responsibilities of a management position.

The SCE policies are mirrored in the positive programmes of other companies. For example, the advantages of promoting from within an organisation are being widely recognised and being seen to bear particularly on the women's situation. One observer, Helen McLane, vice-president of the management consulting firm of Heidrick & Struggles, has noted: 'Progressive firms know that promotion from within means lower turnover of the most able individuals, heightened employee morale, and improved productivity' (quoted in *Computer Decisions*, August 1980). A person from within the organisation is known and understood: this circumstance may induce those who may be reluctant to accept a woman manager to view her more favourably. Elizabeth Shaw Adams, a founder of the Association for Women in Computing, says that 'managers must be convinced that they can grow, train and promote women into the executive dp ranks.' She reckons that the more they do it, the better they'll get at it.

It is clear that various progressive policies are being implemented to help women move into the management ranks of companies and other organisations. The programmes introduced by SCE are not unique and such schemes are bearing fruit. (A spokesperson for the Data Processing Management Association has observed: 'Today, women comprise 15 per cent of our membership, five or ten years ago we were surprised to even get a membership application from a women' – quoted by Snyders and Miles, 1980.) However, it is equally clear that progress is slow, and that the progress of women into dp management and other areas of executive responsibility is hampered by stereotypical views on female characteristics and potential.

FEMALE CHARACTERISTICS, STRESS

The stereotypes prevalent in the culture can be found to influence attitudes in data processing and in management. Margaret Hennig and Anne Jardim pointed out (in *The Managerial Woman*) that wrong attitudes, in both men and women, represent an acute problem at the managerial level. Typical male expectations and definitions of women – wife, mother, lover, etc – can be reinforced by the informal power structure within a company – 'The informal system of relationships finds both its origins and present function in the male culture and in the male experience ... the informal system is truly a bastion of the male life-style.' But for the manager to be successful, it is necessary to cope with the informal system of relationship. This can be difficult for a woman if, by virtue of prevalent stereotypical attitudes, she is effectively excluded from the orbit of informal interactions. Hence, one female executive declares: 'They never invite me to lunch – so I never hear what's going on until they announce it officially. I've arrived, but I'm not equal yet.'

There are a number of assumptions that help to sustain (male and female) attitudes based on stereotypes: for example, that women work only for pin money; that training women is a waste (because they soon leave to have children); that women cannot cope with stress or sudden job crises; that women prefer intellectually undemanding jobs; that women are psychologically unstable or too emotional, and that women are unable or unwilling to travel extensively. Such assumptions are now often referred to as 'myths'.

Hence, according to Bass (1971), woman was downgraded in

business because of four myths:

— She lacks career orientation;

— She lacks supervisory potential,

— She lacks dependability;

— She lacks emotional stability.

In a similar vein, Barbara Wix (Control Data Institut, Frankfurt) indicated, at the International Congress of Data Processing in Berlin (October 1980) what, in her opinion and from her experience, were some of the 'disadvantages' of women. While acknowledging that not all women are the same and that men can have similar faults, she suggested that women —

— are very emotional;

— are inclined to gossip;

— are likely to burst into tears when angry or worried;

— allow curiosity to drive them to rash acts and misplaced enthusiasm;

— have the knack of organising intrigues;

— tend to enter into affairs in the office;

— tend to be jealous of female colleagues;

— transfer their main interest, when they get married, to their husband, with office work becoming a burdensome but necessary subsidiary item;

— are unreliable when pregnant;

— expect the company to take into account a new baby when the woman wants to return to work.

Wix divides the 'disadvantages' into two groups — *emotional* and *family orientation*. Attitudes to such 'disadvantages' are obviously highly relevant to the development of management potential in women. For the purpose of the present chapter we can focus on the idea that women necessarily lack supervisory potential.

It may be implied that women do not welcome responsibility,

promotion or changes in their working patterns that add to their workload. It *may* be thought that there are innate reasons − perhaps related to hormones or brain characteristics − that make women unable to supervise. Such assumptions bear on the acceptability of women for management posts.

Today it is easy to show that the 'supervisory myth' is a clear absurdity. It can quickly be refuted by the abundance of empirical evidence: there are thousands of highly successful female managers in data processing and other industry sectors. Many studies have been conducted to discover the supervisory potential of women, the extent to which they are motivated to progress within a company, or to travel when work requires it. Koff and Handlon (1975), for example, carried out a six-year study of 1775 women in business to discover their motivational attitudes. Nearly a third evinced clear motivation to move upwards in business, with the motivation, in general, unaffected by the level of the women's intelligence, their marital status, or their number of children.

Of the motivated group (30 per cent of the total), three subgroups were identified:

− women who were strong risk-takers, high achievers and very self-confident, and who would pursue goals despite lack of employer support;

− women who would move upward only if there were a positive company climate (deriving from a high company level) that helped them to develop their self-confidence;

− women who would progress if offered a considerable amount of 'hand-holding'. Such women were very security-conscious and needed constant reassurance from their families and from supervisors.

As a matter of self-interest, companies may be expected to develop training and career programmes to advance women from all three categories.

Studies have also focussed on whether women have the ability to manage people. One study (Reif et al, 1975), conducted at the Johnson O'Connor Research Foundation by J J Durkin between 1922 and 1971, was concerned with aptitude differences between

men and women. It was found that in fourteen of the defined aptitudes, some of which are highly relevant to management activity,
there were no differences between men and women. In two aptitudes – grip and structural visualisation – men were superior; and
in no less than six aptitudes women excelled; finger dexterity,
graphoria (accounting ability), ideaphoria (rate of flow of ideas
when talking), observation, silograms (ability to form associations
between words), and abstract visualisations.

Durkin noted various aptitudes that appeared to underlie successful management – those of objective personality, abstract
visualisation and high English vocabulary. Since women were
found to excel in abstract visualisation, Durkin concluded that
there ought to be more women in management than men. And
Reif reports other findings that show that traditional assumptions
that women managers are different (usually meaning inferior) to
their male counterparts are not borne out by the facts. There is no
evidence that women lack supervisory or management abilities.
That women are so poorly represented at the management levels
of companies and other organisations must be attributed to reasons
other than lack of suitable potential.

The other myths – that women lack career orientation, that
they lack dependability or are too emotional, etc – can be subjected to a similar scrutiny. The myths can be shown to be ground-
less, though they serve a psychological purpose – in this case,
often to feed fragile male vanities, and to underwrite traditional
discriminatory attitudes.

The Liebrecht study, already referred to (Delamaide, 1979),
showed that traditional concepts of female qualities still govern
a wide range of attitudes. One question in the study was whether
women are in general as capable as men of fulfilling a leadership
role: 52.7 per cent of the respondents said 'yes', 40.5 per cent res-
ponded 'conditionally', and 6.7 per cent said 'no'. Those with conditional or negative responses were asked why women were less
suitable for management positions. Two-thirds felt that, in general,
women are too strongly influenced by their emotions, and about
the same proportion felt that the double burden of a job and
family is a handicap. It was also suggested that women are less
likely to 'bear up', are less objective, have less ability to follow

things through, and are more likely to be ill. Such views are consistent with prejudices revealed in earlier studies (see, for example, references in Section 5 of Women in Industry, 1980). It should be noted that employers and employees who have had experience of working with women in senior positions tend to have more positive attitudes towards women's management abilities (Hunt, 1975).

The qualities necessary to women who want to progress in management are much the same as a man would need — though some observers have suggested that women should cultivate their female charm for this purpose! A woman executive has declared at a recent workshop on Management Skills for Women: 'I would stress that the five prerequisites for a woman who wants to get ahead in the management field are aggressiveness, ability, aggressiveness, setting of a goal, and aggressiveness.' Such qualities — plus such characteristics as independence and self-reliance — have not traditionally been considered female qualities. However, modern management thinking is tending to emphasise the value of interpersonal sensitivity and concern, qualities that have not been regarded as masculine traits.

When women demonstrate the necessary capabilities and reach the management ranks of a data processing, or other, company, they may have to possess greater capacities to withstand stress than most of their male counterparts. A consensus of American and British research is that the few women who have achieved high-status positions in organisations are likely to experience unique stress and strain not known by male colleagues of the same status (Richbell, 1976; Kanter, 1977). Women in management often have to cope with:

— feelings of isolation;

— burdens of the role of the 'token woman';

— conflicting demands of career and domestic commitments;

— prejudice and stereotyping that lead to covert discrimination from other staff.

One survey of 125 female managers (Davidson and Cooper, 1980), designed to ascertain the specific occupational stresses, covered positions that ranged from company directors and executives to personnel managers, bank managers and engineers. One finding was that only 43 per cent of the sample were married (compared with 65 per cent of the overall female working population in the UK). This marital pattern is similar to that of American women managers who are only a third as likely as their similar-status male colleagues to be married. It has been suggested (Hennig and Jardim, 1979) that women who reject marriage for a career become embittered, depressed and subject to increased stress in later years.

A number of the findings related to levels of perceived stress. It was found that those who thought they were under more stress than peers and superiors saw women as having to cope with more stress than do men in similar positions. (Studies are suggesting that individuals who say they are 'good stress copers' are often high risk in terms of stress-related illnesses.)

Discriminatory pressures are increasingly being recognised as a source of stress to women managers (and to other working women). The vast majority of American women managers surveyed have reported having been discriminated against at some time. The UK Department of Employment found a number of discriminatory attitudes and practices in the working environment. These related to hours of work, geographical mobility, length of service, and male-oriented career routes.

As many as 74 per cent of the women managers in the Davidson/ Cooper study reported discriminatory practices: for example, for equally qualified men and women, it has been usual for men to be promoted more rapidly. Looking at only the last two or three years, 56 per cent of the women managers thought that this still applied. This circumstance may be interpreted as a stress factor with which women subject to discrimination have to contend.

The stress factors which bear uniquely on women managers may be expected to have various consequences. Women may be deterred from seeking, or retaining, managerial posts. They may be prevented from accepting promotion to the ranks of senior management. And there may be consequences for physical and mental health — which in turn are likely to affect performance and promotional prospects.

The overall situation facing women executives is one in which discriminatory pressures can, in some ways, be felt more than by women at lower levels in an organisation. The female manager tends to get little support from female peers — since there are very few around. And there are the usual problems associated with prejudice and stereotyping. Again, a consequence is that, in order to be taken seriously, the female executive has to be more competent and better qualified than her male counterparts.

Female managers in the data processing industry have to contend with the sorts of problems discussed above — but there may be additional difficulties associated with the technical nature of computing. However technically competent a woman is, there will still be stereotypical attitudes evident in colleagues: for example, women are supposed to be less technically proficient than men — though this type of prejudice is more likely to bear on the female hardware specialist than on the female programmer or systems analyst. The female dp manager, who may be expected to have both hardware and software experience, is likely to be subject to traditional prejudice in one form or another.

Information drawn from a 1979 *Computerworld* survey showed the typical female data processing manager (in the US) to be college-educated, to have spent most of her working career in data processing, and to have spent several years in the same company working her way up to the management ranks. Typically the woman data processing administrator has not married or is divorced, and is in her thirties.

Forty per cent of the women surveyed began their careers as trainees (usually in programming); and 28 per cent started as programmers. There was no evident link between educational background and the women's starting positions. The other respondents began as key-punchers or in a variety of other jobs. The women had worked in dp for between five and thirty years (14.9 years average). On average it took the women 8.4 years before they were promoted to management. And they believed that in their management positions they encountered much less discrimination than they did in their former non-management positions.

Again there seems to be difficulty in reconciling a position in dp management with domestic commitment. More than half the women surveyed were single, divorced or separated. However, there are signs that the situation is changing, ie that stress and domestic problems may be coming to afflict male and female data processing managers more equally. One women interviewed, a senior vice-president, declared that there was no discrimination in data processing (quoted in *Computerworld*, 5/3/79), and that 'the fellows are beginning to feel they're getting the short shrift.'

PROFILES OF FEMALE MANAGERS

Though discrimination is evident at all levels of the data processing industry, many women (though few proportionally) have succeeded in progressing into management. Respondents in the *Computerworld* survey suggested that the situation is opening up, and that there is more improvement in the dp management job category than in any other. More women are being noticed, not just in programming and systems analysis, but also in such areas as sales and computer operations — areas formerly more or less closed to women. The headline 'Opportunities Opening Up' (*Computerworld*, 5/3/79) conveys what is certainly a widespread, if misleading, impression about the data processing industry.

In the US, women have been increasingly able to set up their own businesses ('commentators are claiming that the '80s will be the decade of the woman entrepreneur ... women have been able to set up their own businesses, winning the backing of bankers and venture capitalists' — Lamb, 1980). Paradoxically, discrimination within large companies is one of the key factors encouraging women to set up their own businesses: if the progress of an ambitious woman in data processing is artificially blocked, she may have no recourse but to create her own company.

Sandra Kurtzig, for example, president of ASK Computer Services, started the firm nine years ago with $2000 of her own money. The company, still 95 per cent owned by Kurtzig, now turns over more than $2 million and has licensed its production control system to Sperry Univac. A $1 million joint venture has been negotiated with another electronics company. Kurtzig has a master's degree in aeronautical engineering and four years' experience in computer operations with TR and General Electric.

Another company, Vector Graphic, currently turning over

$18 million a year is run by Lore Harp and Carole Ely. The two
women began by selling a memory board, and now have a workforce of well over a hundred, and a dealership network with 225
outlets marketing their business machines. Harp, president of
Vector Graphic, hopes to develop the company further by turning
Vector Graphic into a public corporation.

It has also been emphasised that there is prejudice against
women trying to raise capital ('The first-time business woman
must work hard to convince predominantly male financiers of her
worth'). Harp commonly works twelve hours a day, and Kurtzig
estimates that she puts in about 80 hours a week. To an extent
this sort of commitment is essential to any entrepreneur, male or
female, trying to establish and develop a young company in a hostile economic climate.

Despite the evident success stories, women entrepreneurs and
managers are still rare (see also the profiles in Chapter 1). One article (*Data Processing*, January 1981, pp 12-13) begins: 'Women
data processing managers are almost as rare as System 38s, which
is a shame, although it's probably an accurate reflection of the
numbers of women managers in most industries, not just data processing.' (The same writer notes the frequent references – by
newspaper and magazine writers, press officers, commentators and
others – to 'punch girls' and 'data prep girls', while it is assumed
that managerial and senior positions will be held by men.)

Miriam Macdonald is profiled (in *Data Processing*) as one of the
few women to have become data processing managers. She says: 'I
don't understand why there aren't more women dp managers. It's
a sad state of affairs when you think about the numbers of women
in the industry.' For three years, Macdonald has been data processing manager for the Civil Service Building Society, set up in 1932 to
help lower-paid civil servants to obtain mortgages. There are now
total assets of £22 million, 10,000 investors, 2,500 mortgages and
a staff complement of about thirty.

Macdonald has just one programmer and two operators to help
her to look after an NCR 8250 minicomputer. Macdonald is currently exploring word processing possibilities. She began working
life as an accounts clerk, then joined NCR where she first learned
programming and then progressed to project leader. At that time

she worked in conjunction with the sales team and looked after new installations, sometimes as many as twelve at a time. At one stage she had to evaluate a package that NCR was selling to the Civil Service Building Society — which is how she came into contact with her present company.

When she joined the society, Macdonald worked for two years to specify and write her own system. She was helped by two freelance programmers and a mature TOPS graduate. Today she is able to relax slightly, occupied solely by day-to-day running and maintenance of the system, management activities, and her research into word processing. She is a member of the IDPM and of the NCR user group.

Sometimes women progress to the level of data processing manager without being aware of any discrimination on the way. Marion Carney, for example, became dp manager at Richard Costain, and does not feel that there is any prejudice towards her as a woman. She joined ICL (then ICT) as a trainee programmer, after two years moving to BICC as a programmer. She then joined Costain as a systems analyst and design trainee.

Carney did not originally aspire to management ('I am the type of person who likes to do a job well, and I'm flexible about accepting different responsibilities as they come along'). She emphasises the value of good communication, including trust and having respect for others' opinions. This accords with survey findings that suggest that women in management often present a more 'human' face to subordinates than do male counterparts.

Christine Stott, sales promotion manager at Case, the communications systems supplier, has emphasised that women must take a realistic attitude towards their career if they wish to be promoted. For example, they must work long hours where necessary ('they must take the same attitude as men do if they expect the same rewards'). Stott began work as a technical officer at the Chemical Warfare Establishment at Porton Down. After a period at the Lister Institute, she moved to a recruiting position with a scientific personnel agency, where she developed an interest in computer staff recruitment. She was then offered a position as a call dispatcher in the Case field engineering department, which mainly entailed dealing with customer problems. Stott, like many successful women in the data processing industry, appears to have no particular ideological axe to grind ('I suppose I am a chauvinist in reverse').

It may be significant that successful dp women often appear largely oblivious to discriminatory pressures. Perhaps such women have progressed in a relatively enlightened environment, or perhaps they possess personal qualities that allow them to brush aside discriminatory constraints. They may also feel that being a woman has certain advantages (Sonya Howell Jones: 'If you have sound reasoning and good judgement, you can use your charm as the final straw'). One observer (Harvey, 1978) found that women whom she interviewed believed that women had a highly developed understanding of people and that this helped them in problem-solving situations. Carney believes that this is an advantage in her position, since judging people is an integral part of sorting out problems. But she has still detected the discriminatory pressure — everyone who would be working for her was asked by management if they would object to working for a woman ('Even my secretary ... was asked by personnel if she objected to working for a woman').

Prejudice against women in computing is well documented, though its character has changed over the history of the industry (Walsh, 1977). Similar patterns emerge repeatedly: double standards are used in judging men and women; women have to be better qualified than men to be treated on a basis of equality; and artificial barriers constrain the progress of women into senior management ranks. Walsh, involved in the industry since 1955, concludes: 'A large number of women I have met and with whom I have worked have made significant contributions to the development of the technology and its application. They have demonstrated a capacity for technical and administrative management as well as for technical and administrative detail. They have shown once again that being wives and/or mothers doesn't affect their ability to do the job... They have shown that in dealing with men in sales, technical and managerial areas their sex does not diminish their contribution.'

It is obvious that there are relatively few women managers in the data processing industry. The success of a handful of highly talented women in this area cannot be interpreted as signalling a situation of equal opportunities. However, there is a developing consciousness that women can contribute significantly in this area as elsewhere — and each new success story adds plausibility to the broad feminist claims. Progress is being made. Women are encroaching on many formerly all-male preserves. (As one example, in 1980 Elizabeth Payne was elected the first woman member of the executive council of the IDPM.) Continued progress demands, not only the sustained enthusiasm and motivation of women, but sensible company policies designed to exploit a greatly under-used human resource.

STEPS TO TAKE

We have seen that most companies, in the UK and elsewhere, feel that no particular steps should be taken to advance the position of women, that in fact any such programme could itself be interpreted as discriminatory (and indeed there may be some support for this view in the specific working of the UK Sex Discrimination Act). However, it is not true that women are competing in a situation of equal opportunities. It is hard to avoid the conclusion that some steps should be taken by managements to redress the balance, and that such an approach is in the interest of both the personnel and the companies concerned.

In 1978, an EOC survey of current practices of 500 leading UK companies found that only 25 per cent of respondents had a formal policy statement bearing on equal opportunities. In July 1979 the CBI issued a statement supporting the principle of equal opportunities in employment and encouraging constructive equal opportunities policies. This was accompanied by guidelines on general principles and practice. The statutory duties of employers with regard to discrimination were outlined, and a list was provided of possible contents for equal-opportunity policies and conditions for effective policy operation.

Some companies have been more sensitive to the requirements than others. A 1975 working party in ICI considered the company's record in female employment and whether this national resource was being adequately developed. A code urging improvements in job appraisal and training was later distributed to ICI managers. It is expected that more female ICI employees will move into middle management over the next few years. Other employers cited (eg in *Women in Industry*, 1980) as forward-looking in this area include the Camden and Hackney Borough Councils, J Sainsbury Ltd and Barclays Bank International.

The industrial training boards have initiated schemes specifically designed for women. And the training services division of the Man-power Services Commission (MSC), which helps to coordinate the ITBs, has sponsored a research programme on women and manage-ment (held at the Ashridge Management Centre). One aim is to produce a package of guidelines to help companies in analysing factors that limit the progress of women in employment.

There are a number of steps that companies can take to bring more women into management in data processing and other ind-ustry sectors. Eleanor Macdonald, founder of *Women in Manage-ment*, has suggested that companies should stop writing endless reports which quote 'often irrelevant statistics' and should imple-ment a few well thought out plans. There should be targets and target dates, with top management clearly being seen to support the plans. It is likely that changes will be involved in recruitment patterns, training policies, and career pathing. Organisations should not delude themselves that women 'don't want promotion!' The brightest do — 'and it's those who are worth taking trouble with.'

Macdonald also suggests that government departments and agencies should set a lead, ensuring that appropriate training is introduced, career paths structured, and an atmosphere created that may be expected to influence the behaviour of companies. Further, the British Institute of Management should run seminars and invite women speakers — real experts, not just 'token' women — to attend. Membership privileges could be given to aspiring women, such as access to the library. It is likely that such plans would help to motivate women, to develop the self-confidence and positive self-image that would aid personal progress and the succ-ess of company enterprises.

In a similar spirit it has been suggested (*EDP Analyzer* August 1976) that changes should occur on three corporate levels. Efforts should be made to:

— *create a positive corporate environment.* This requires the commitment of top management, and such steps as the implementation of a programme to monitor the compliance of middle managers, the appointment of an executive to analyse company policies, and the introduction of training schemes.

— *to alter ('resocialise') men's attitudes.* Steps need to be taken to alter traditional male attitudes, eg awareness courses can be introduced, inviting discussion and a scrutiny of prejudice, stereotyping and other irrational attitudes. And managers need to be helped 'in working with women'.

— *train women for management.* Companies should encourage women to take training to improve their self-image, to learn self-motivation, and to develop management skills. In the US there are consultants, seminars, films and university courses available to help managements to develop such programmes.

Management development programmes should also be framed to help both men and women overcome what may be seen as role difficulties. One observer (Koehn, 1976) has indicated what the programme should contain for women:

— Stereotypes (eg that women lack ambition) should be exposed;

— Management jobs should be structured to eliminate irrelevant sex typing and qualifications;

— Performance goals should be objectively defined;

— Team-building skills should be developed;

— Assistance should be provided for career planning;

— Women should be trained 'to solve conflicts through informal methods, to manage conflict constructively without negative feelings';

— Special emphasis should be placed on the importance of understanding the corporate structure.

Various writers have emphasised that special treatment for women (whether managers or not) can adversely affect the working atmosphere (Trish Hendershot, employee development co-ordinator in the Office of Operations and Finance, US Department of Agriculture: 'Treating women managers specially only fosters resentment. Women are no more special than anyone else'). At the same time it is clear how women managers should *not* be treated (Snyders and Miles, 1980):

- She should be treated the same as a male manager, not given 'superstar' status;
- She should not be eliminated from male-dominated discuss-ions;
- It should not be assumed that women are unable to address a group of men, to chair committees, or to handle travel plans, noisy workplaces and late hours;
- A woman's leadership qualities should not be prejudged. If stereotyping influences judgement of a woman then her per-formance will be adversely affected;
- Women should be allowed to develop their own style of leadership. They should not be excessively controlled or directed;
- Women should not be designated 'managers' if in fact they are not, ie they should not be patronised.

Many of the steps that companies could take to advance women in data processing and other areas seem largely a matter of common sense. It may be seen as highly significant that measures as transparently obvious as these are implemented so rarely by company managements, or with such evident lack of enthusiasm in most cases. It is also clear that companies are neglecting a vital resource that could aid their commercial viability. They would be very reluctant to neglect in this way any other company resource.

SUMMARY

As in other areas of female employment there is evidence of dis-crimination against women aspiring to be managers in the data processing, or any other, industry. And there are signs that women managers, by virtue of their relative isolation, face particular prob-lems. The difficulties that female data processing managers, or women executives in computing companies, have to contend with may be exacerbated by the technical nature of the industry ('women are not supposed to be technical'). But successful entrepreneurial and managerial women are, by achieving personal success, adding credibility to the feminist demands for equal treatment, and at the same time helping to erode traditional prejudice.

Various companies in the US, the UK and elsewhere are taking steps to frame equal opportunities programmes. In such organisations there is sensitivity to equal opportunities legislation and to the legitimate demands of employed women. In other organisations there is reluctance to introduce programmes specifically designed for women. This can be construed, in many cases, as a neglect of important company and national resources.

4 The Office Environment

INTRODUCTION

One of the most important consequences of developments in microelectronics is increased automation in offices (see, for example, Price, 1979). The microprocessor is being progressively introduced into this environment, and office workers are being confronted with a growing range of computer-based systems. New products are being announced weekly, with consequences for business programmes, office activities, and the employment of clerical and other staff.

The 1970 TUC annual report observed that 'the introduction of the computer did not appear to have resulted in any overall decrease in staff.' At that time, despite alarmist predictions, the computer impact on employment was not thought to be a problem area. But with the emergence of the new micro-based products, bearing particularly on the office environment of the 1970s, the employment issue became a matter of growing concern. And it became increasingly apparent that women were most affected by the steady movement towards office automation.

The 'shunting' of women into low-grade office jobs — as clerks, typists, junior administrators, etc — meant that *they* would be most affected by the introduction of computer-based systems in the business environment. Today more and more business systems, word processing devices and other office units are becoming commercially available. We are finding a growing range of automatic text processing units, facsimile equipment, microfilm retrieval/ updating systems, automated filing systems, electronic diaries, etc, being used in offices. By 1980 the word processing market in the

US had reached well over $100 million, with around 20,000 work-stations in operation, and there were significant developments in other areas that received less publicity. Microprocessors are finding their way into an increasing number of office units, with the result that many tasks formerly performed by (usually female) low-grade labour can now be carried out automatically.

Apart from the evident growth in the number of word process-ing systems commercially available (see, for example, NCC *Computer Hardware Record*), a range of other office tools are being provided with microprocessor-based intelligence. And micros are moving into copiers, duplicators and guillotines to simplify opera-tional tasks, and to reduce the amount of training needed by staff. For example, a built-in microcomputer in the Rank Xerox 9400 copier provides automatic fault-diagnosis and memory facilities to chart the state of a job. Similarly the Canon NP80 plain-paper copier automatically maintains copy quality. Guillotines (eg the Camco 825MP device) carry microprocessors to aid the sequencing of complex cutting sequences.

The consequences of these technological developments bear mainly on women. It is relatively easy to replace low-grade staff, performing routine tasks, by economic computer-based systems. And where female staff are retained, they often find that their job satisfaction has diminished, that their work has been 'deskilled' by the introduction of intelligent electronic equipment. The deskill-ing process has always received less publicity than the threat posed to jobs by new technology. For example, there have been many disputes, in the UK and elsewhere, about how word processors may threaten (mainly female) jobs. As one instance, in February 1979 the Bradford branch of NALGO was involved in a dispute about the likely impact of word processors. It was suggested that 18 or 19 copy typists' jobs were lost when Word-Plex equipment was introduced in June 1977. In November 1978 NALGO rejected plans to introduce a word processor system in the Bradford educa-tion department, fearing that another 90 jobs might be lost.

Women work with computers mostly in the office environment. Modern electronic systems are increasingly microprocessor-based, and a clerk may operate a copier or an office guillotine without realising that such devices may contain microcomputer systems.

But the low-grade character of most female office work means that the interaction with computer-based systems is not always a happy one. The new technology has brought to office staff – mainly women – the threat of redundancy, the possibility of job deskilling, and certain health hazards. The *benefits* of the new technology (eg increased office efficiency, enhanced company viability, etc) are more likely to affect men than women. It is a mark of the business culture that where technology brings disadvantages these largely afflict women, whereas men mostly experience the advantages. Few people could deny that this situation is evidence for discrimination in the modern office environment.

DISCRIMINATION

A number of studies have shown that the introduction of new technology, in the context of a deepening economic recession, is affecting women more than men, and that this disproportionate impact will continue through the 1980s. For example, the study by Emma Bird (1980) predicts that one consequence of the new computer-based technology will be the loss of up to 170,000 typing and secretarial jobs in Britain – 17 per cent of the total – by 1990. The report suggests that by 1985, 21,000 jobs will have disappeared because of the introduction of word processors. And the job market is shrinking even more rapidly for clerks than for typists and secretaries.

It is emphasised that automation is bringing a permanent shift in white-collar work from the low-paid, semi-skilled jobs to more senior posts requiring higher educational and professional qualifications, ie from traditional female jobs to traditional male jobs. The study found no evidence in Britain to support the argument that office automation will increase the opportunities for secretaries to move into management. In fact in one company, mentioned in the report, personal secretaries were worried by the removal of the typing load because there was no other work available. The company's solution was to reclass the personal secretary as 'administrative secretary' – answerable to several managers rather than just to one.

The scale of economic recession (for example, with UK registered unemployment exceeding 10% in March 1981) has tended to obscure the disproportionate burdens carried by different parts of the country and by different job sectors. It has also obscured the fact that women — who often do not register at the labour exchanges — are being harder hit than men. Apart from being under greater threat of redundancy, they are finding it hard to retain the steps made towards equal opportunity in the employment that does survive. Where labour — male or female — is insecure, as in the present economic circumstances, traditional employment patterns and prejudices tend to be sustained. In practical terms it is harder to argue for equal opportunities when *all* jobs are at risk. Rising (male and female) unemployment is likely to fuel discriminatory pressures.

THE IMPACT OF OFFICE AUTOMATION

We have suggested that office automation has a unique impact on the situation of women in employment. Three specific areas where this is the case can be highlighted:

- *Employment.* Is the introduction of computer-based systems in the office environment disproportionately affecting women in terms of job insecurity, redundancy, etc? What are the trends?

- *Job deskilling.* As women increasingly work with computer-based systems in offices, are their jobs deskilled, with consequences for morale, job satisfaction, motivation, etc?

- *Health.* Are there factors in the new technology that affect health? To what extent have these been allowed for in devising office routines and other working practices?

Employment

In the UK more than 70 per cent of employed women are in the service industries. No less than two out of five of all women workers are employed in low-grade low-salary occupations — as clerks, typists, secretaries, office machine operators, telephonists and such like. It is obvious that what is happening with office automation is of crucial concern to women.

Companies are growing increasingly sensitive to office costs. In one estimate, the cost of running offices amounts to half of the total operating costs of all US corporations. And in government and service industries, such as banking and insurance, the office wage bill can amount to three-quarters of total running costs. In the UK, wages now account for 80 per cent of all office costs. It is hardly surprising, in these circumstances, that corporate managements are scrutinising office expenditure with a view to economies and more efficient investment. (However, sometimes the resulting policies are misplaced. In a typical organisation in which there is one secretary to every five managers, with managers paid twice as much as secretarial staff, a 30 per cent increase in secretarial productivity is equivalent to an overall saving of only 3 per cent – a benefit that could be wiped out by an increased need for messengers and clerks, and wasted executive activity.)

An obvious way for managers to improve office efficiency is to install cost-effective equipment that can replace relatively expensive staff. There are already more than 9000 word processors installed in the UK, with a growing market. One consequence is that fewer jobs are required in many business sectors. The suppliers of word processors claim that the average typist or secretary spends only 30 to 35 per cent of her time at the typewriter, with a high proportion of this time spent retyping corrected drafts, standard letters and forms. It is suggested that the introduction of word processors can achieve cost savings of 50 to 100 per cent. Logica, distributor of the UNICOM system, has claimed productivity increases of up to 400 per cent – or one typist doing the work of as many as five using conventional equipment.

Many organisations have introduced word processors with an increase in productivity which may or may not have led to loss of jobs. The Provident Financial Group installed three IBM memory typewriters into their typing pool. Full-time typing staff were reduced from 27 to 17, part-time staff from 13 to 3, and the workload was increased. The Halifax Building Society moved from automatic typewriters to 16 IBM word processors, resulting in no loss of jobs but a workload that almost trebled. The National Coal Board installed word processors on a pilot basis at Staffordshire House, reducing staff through natural wastage from 20 to 14. And the Central Electricity Generating Board has reduced its staff at the Bristol typing centre from 50 to 26. Such examples are typical of the impact of word processors in many industry and business sectors.

A large number of women's jobs have already been lost through the introduction of word processors, but the high turnover of many low-grade office staff has often allowed managers to opt for a 'natural wastage' solution. This inevitably means a loss of job opportunities for women coming onto the labour market. Where companies have achieved an expanding business activity — rare in the present commercial climate — they have not reduced their staffing levels but increased output many times over.

The natural-wastage solution plus redeployment has enabled managements largely to avoid labour-relations problems and confrontations with trade unions, but the upshot is still loss of jobs. Often the job loss in any one organisation is small (for example, when the British Standards Institute created a specialist word processing department, the number of employed typists and secretaries fell by a third), but the total effect is considerable when the process is repeated thousands of times throughout a national economy. APEX, the office workers union, using a conservative approach, has predicted that word processors will lead to office job losses of 250,000 by 1983. And the NORA report (1978) for the French government predicted that modern computer technology in banking could reduce staff in this sector by 30 per cent over the next ten years.

In a late-1979 survey, fourteen UK word processing installations were studied, some of which are among the largest and most experienced in the country. In as many as 12 of the 14 cases, the typing and secretarial jobs were reduced by between 3 and 73 per cent following the introduction of word processing. Productivity increases were recorded for all 14 cases, ranging from 10 to 300 per cent. Such findings (reported by McMahon, 1980) accord with other trend forecasts made by both private and government groups. For instance, a report from Siemens predicts that by 1990, 40 per cent of Germany's 5 million typing and secretarial jobs could be carried out by computer-based systems. (Siemens, in fact, makes the machines that will help to cause the 40 per cent job loss.)

One London company reduced its typing staff by more than 66 per cent over a two-year period, following the introduction of word processing. Redundancies were avoided, the reduction being achieved entirely through natural wastage. Another multinational company based in London found that word processing systems enabled them to keep pace with an increasing workload without increasing their staff quota — whereas they were accustomed to taking on around 60 extra typists a year. At the Automobile Association, shortage of space plus an increased workload made the company move to a centralised word processing system. A productivity increase of 25 per cent was accompanied by a reduction of staff from 25 to seven typists over a three-year period.

(The 1979 survey of 14 word processor installations found what Emma Bird was to confirm in the more detailed 1980 study: there was no evidence that freeing typists from a proportion of their mundane duties encouraged them to move into management. In all of the 14 case studies, women were supervisors of the word processor installations, but the more senior position of word processing manager was invariably held by a man. Some of the former typists were renamed 'administrative secretaries', and others were required to do the drudgery typing — further evidence of job deskilling.)

It has been apparent for some time that female unemployment in the UK is rising faster than male unemployment. Figures for the period 1974 to 1978 (source: DE Gazette, August 1978) show the female increase to be three times as rapid as the male. This is despite the fact that, for several reasons, the figures for women are generally conservative. The job market is shrinking in many traditionally female areas, only one of which is the office environment. Women's share of professional jobs, ie those that may best weather an economic recession, is extremely low, only the professions of dentist and general practitioner being more than ten per cent female.

The rising levels of unemployment in the UK and elsewhere have made more acute the fears that women's job opportunities may be further restricted by the introduction of computer-based systems. There is no automatic positive correlation between increases in productivity — to which microelectronics developments may be expected to contribute — and decreases in unemployment. (In fact, in today's economic climate we are likely to think that there is a negative correlation: 'increased productivity' often appears as a synonym for 'increased unemployment'.)

Emma Bird studied a number of organisations to evaluate the impact of word processors on employment and other aspects. It was found, for example, that two users achieved productivity gains of one hundred per cent or more: a chemical company division and a public administration department increased their workload, at the same time reducing staff by fifty per cent. In another case — the headquarters of the chemical company — 20 jobs out of 300 were lost, coupled with a productivity gain of seven per cent. And this experience highlights a typical circumstance in the introduction of word processing systems. A detailed feasibility study inevitably precedes the introduction of word processors — and the study itself often indicates how staff savings can be achieved, independent of the acquisition of new equipment. Job loss can occur because of the rationalisation within the organisation, not solely because of the introduction of word processors. And staff changes can generate a rationalisation momentum. In three of the organisations where typing and secretarial jobs were lost, there were plans to reduce the establishment levels for clerks, typists and secretaries still more in the future.

We have seen that 'natural wastage' rather than redundancy can be used to reduce jobs. Four of the organisations studied by Emma Bird had a 'no-redundancy' agreement with their staff, and two of the organisations that had agreed a redundancy scheme with staff had no cause to use it in the case of jobs removed by the introduction of word processors. The organisations were able to implement their plans via natural wastage and redeployment. And two of the major users of word processors kept the same number of staff to cope with an increased workload. It was found that word processors led to a reduction of jobs in three of the nine case studies. The APEX statement ('the ability of word processor systems ... to replace typists at least on a one for one basis seems virtually indisputable') is relevant in only a proportion of cases.

There can be little doubt that word-processor usage will increase through the 1980s. There are evident cost savings and productivity gains in this approach, though conservatism and the state of the UK economy may restrict the rate of implementation. In one estimate (Bird, 1980), there will be a steady growth of word processors* up to the mid-1980s: 26,400 (1981), 32,000 (1982), 41,200 (1983), 51,900 (1984) and 64,000 (1985) — compared with an installed base of 10,000 word processors in 1975. It is partly on this basis that a likely job loss by 1990 of 170,000 — seventeen per cent of all typing and secretarial jobs — is estimated.

Clerical jobs, again mostly staffed by women, will also be under increasing threat from the introduction of word processors and other computer-based equipment. Increasing automation may be expected in such clerical tasks as data preparation, the processing of orders and insurance premiums, payroll preparation, stock control, low-grade banking and accounting jobs, etc. Predictions of the consequences of microelectronics for employment in these and other areas are contained in various recent reports (Table 12).

Report	Type of Jobs Affected	Number
Siemens, 1978	40% office jobs computerised by 1990 (Germany)	Two million typing and secretarial jobs
Nora & Minc, May 1978	Banking and insurance jobs (France)	30% reduction in jobs over next decade
APEX, March 1979	Typing, secretarial, clerical, etc Authors of letters & documents	250,000 jobs by 1983
Barron & Curnow 1979	Secretarial, typing, clerical and managerial	10-20% unemployment over the next 15 years
Jenkins and Sherman, 1979	Information processing jobs	30% displacement by 1990
Virgo, 1979	Clerical, administrative (insurance, banking, building societies, etc)	40% jobs at risk in 1980s
Sleigh at al, 1979	Clerical, administrative (banking, insurance, etc)	Modest changes in employment patterns

Table 12   Forecasts of Microelectronics Impact on Job Sectors

* defined as typewriters with sufficient storage and intelligence to permit the modification and output of two or more pages of stored text; a higher forecast if electronic typewriters with limited revision capability are included.

Bird (1980) cites instances of clerical job losses caused through the introduction of new technology. It is also noted that where a loss of clerical jobs leads to the creation of new jobs, the new positions tend to be more senior (eg in programming, systems analysis or management), ie there is a shift of jobs from the traditional female areas to areas that are more likely to be staffed by men. It is rare in such circumstances for new clerical or secretarial jobs to be created.

Word processors can be used to eliminate a range of intermediate text-handling clerical jobs. For example, at Willis Faber (discussed in the 'Apex View of Office Technology', 1979) a Wang machine is pre-programmed, and then used to balance the percentage of insurance risk taken by insurance companies and Lloyd's syndicates in offering cover. The system makes the necessary calculations, retrieves coded details of all participants stored in the system, and then prints out slips to notify them of the final percentage of risk that they have taken. Finally, formats are retrieved and other documentation sent out as required. Hence the system performs a range of tasks previously carried out by a large number of clerks with varying duties.

It may be expected that the introduction of computer-based systems will reduce the need for clerks, typists and secretaries in the 1980s, particularly in circumstances of economic recession. Inevitably this will mostly affect women's jobs, creating higher levels of observable unemployment and higher levels of disguised unemployment (where women do not register at the labour exchanges or do not seek work in a discouraging job climate). Trade unions (eg APEX, ASTMS, CPSA, SOGAT, etc) are well aware of these developments, and in the main have avoided neo-Luddite responses, seeking instead consultation and the framing of technology agreements. Such efforts are highly relevant to the job security of women confronted with computer-based systems in the office environment.

Job Deskilling

It is often claimed that word processors have 'deskilling' consequences for office jobs, and that this has effects on morale, job satisfaction, and motivation. Again the deskilling affects traditional women's jobs: it is rarely assumed that *men* will be the new word-processor operators in companies introducing computer-based technology.

To a large extent word-processor manufacturers *intend* that office jobs should be deskilled by their products. It is taken as an important sales feature that a new word processor can be used 'by anyone, however small their IQ' (Parks, 1980). Salesmen claim that anyone can use the new systems ('even the silliest girl in your typing pool'). At the recent business-machine exhibitions at the Cunard Hotel, Hammersmith, salesmen instructed obedient girls what to do when a demonstration was required. Parks: '... the boss is impressed. The technology has now been especially fashioned to dovetail with the social structure as he knows it.' And a salesman is quoted, with regard to one commercial system, on how the processor is split into two parts (with a typewriter keyboard on one side and special function keys on the other) — 'Your girl can operate the word-processing facility most of the day, and then when your man from accounts wants some data processing done he can pop down for an hour or so and do it himself while the girl handles the post. There's no need for her to know anything about that!'

When the Central Electricity Generating Board reduced its number of girls at the typing centre in Bristol from more than 50 to 26, following the introduction of word processors, a supervisor commented that 'a less experienced typist is able to produce the same quality of work as a really skilled girl and about as quickly.' In a recent CIS report, *The New Technology*, another observer is quoted as noting that 'among the subsidiary benefits management expects to derive from (office automation) is the reduction and thus cheapening of the skills of administrative employees...' For this reason, the new word-processor systems are designed to require little training (eg Wang claims that its System 30, a visual word processor, 'requires minimum operator training for maximum productivity').

Many word-processor manufacturers have, over recent years, dramatically simplified the operation of their products (Krass, 1980). A consequence is that today word-processor operators require fewer skills than their immediate predecessors, and so less training is required. Sometimes the only training deemed necessary is a set of self-instruction leaflets provided with the equipment. Thus IBM provides 'self-paced literature' for the Displaywriter, most people learning the complete operation of the system in about five days. ('The Displaywriter will be easy to learn, so we won't provide any stand-up training.')

Karen Nussbaum, executive director of Working Women (an American office workers association), has commented that operating word processors may not be a health hazard (see below) but it is dull and does lessen workers' job satisfaction. In a similar vein, Philip Kraft, a sociologist at the State University of New York, notes that the introduction of word processors 'is an attempt to industrialise white collar workers in the same way we industrialised craftsmen and artisans in the past.' The aim is to 'replace skilled people with skilled machines tended by unskilled people.' This in turn will lead to further worker polarisation in the office environment — technicians, programmers and designers (the 'smart' people) on the one hand; and machine-minders on the other. Kraft sees 'stupid workers and smart machines' being the goal for every manager in the workplace. Philip Dorn, a New York Office automation consultant, sees office automation as pushing those at the bottom of society out of work, a circumstance that will be encouraged by job polarisation. A recent (late-1980) correspondent, after speaking to people (operators, managers, supervisors and personnel officers) who work with word processors, noted that there are already two classes of word-processor operators — programmers, systems analysts, policy makers ('who love the things'); and the secretaries who would 'otherwise be found in a typing pool' (Warr, 1980).

Most of the women required to operate new word processing equipment are not given new career possibilities. It has been suggested that a few 'token' women escape from the secretarial pool to become administrators, relieved by word processing of the 'drudgery' typing. But this typing is still carried out by the majority, often in what amounts to a production line atmosphere. Karen Nussbaum: 'Although many people like the new machines when they make work easier or more enjoyable, in some cases the rewards of clerical work are eliminated. Work is being broken into more specialised jobs that are often boring and highly repetitive.

And the rewards, pride in a job well done, meeting other people in the company, following through on a task from beginning to end, are removed.' Over-specialisation in the work of typists can lead to morale problems. One aim of word processing configurations is to keep typists at their machines for a greater proportion of the working day. In such circumstances it is important to keep their work varied and interesting.

In the Emma Bird study (1980), seven out of nine management interviewees thought that the word-processor operators found the job more satisfying than the copy typist job. Three aspects were seen as contributing to job satisfaction:

— reduction of standard-text repetitive work;

— high speed of throughput;

— quality of output.

In two of the cases, the university department and the research consultancy, an absence of job satisfaction was reported. Here an absence of a skilled word-processor operator caused problems: management was unable to determine whether the operator was incompetent or whether the machine was faulty.

Twenty-six out of 51 equipment operators reported that their job now had more variety and nearly three-quarters (36) stated that they had more job satisfaction. This finding can be interpreted in various ways. The new job satisfaction could be a temporary phenomenon associated with the novelty of the technology and the newly-acquired status of operators; or the job may carry increased responsibility. APEX has argued that the positive reaction from a proportion of the typists moved to word processing is a short-time phenomenon, with the disadvantages of a highly-specialised activity likely to become apparent in the long term.

Criticism of the Bird study (eg as reported by Church, 1980) suggests that — for example, in the case of bank tellers — not enough effort was made to solicit an alternative view from staff or from their union. Hence Lynette Savings (secretary of the equal opportunities committee of the Banking, Insurance and Finance Union, Bifu): '...we would stress that the perception of job satisfaction, skills required and promotion prospects would tend to reflect the current market situation in which word processor operators are at a premium, and would be very different where the use of word processors was widespread and commonplace.' And Savings notes the possibility also suggested by other observers, that of an unbridgeable gap developing between wp operators and administrative secretaries.

It has been suggested that the deskilling caused by the introduction of word processors is one of the factors influencing job satisfaction and morale. (For example, a word-processor operator does not need to learn how to indent, justify or tabulate — at present, crucial elements in a typing course. By pressing a few keys, the machine will do it all.) Another factor is the extent to which operators feel that they are being monitored by management.

Employers must be attracted by the possibility that word processors will increase their control in the office environment. There is the suggestion that 'a word processor or accounting machine not only increases the productivity of the operator: it also divests the operator of control over his or her own labour' (CIS Report, *The New Technology*). The machines can be paced and controlled according to centralised decisions: this is clearly of interest to management. Bird points out that 'shared logic systems automatically count keystrokes over time,' thus highlighting the possibility of efficient supervision that may not be recognised by the operator. (Such monitoring facilities are sometimes linked to provisions allowing the machine to evaluate the operator's activities and to respond. For example, 'screen prompts' can tell the operator what to do next.) Typical advertising copy from Wang indicates the intention of the new monitoring facilities: 'A built-in reporting system helps you monitor your work flow. It automatically gives the author and typist's name, the document number, the date and time of last revision, the required editing time, and the length of the document.' Of the Dictaphone Corporation's systems, Timemaster and Mastermind, the company claims: 'They give all that a good supervisor would know, but now electronically. You couldn't fail to get work on time.'

Word processors are designed to improve office productivity. They can represent highly efficient systems with a wide range of important and cost-effective facilities. At the same time, they tend to deskill jobs and to lead to 'conveyor-belt' typing. Operators may find themselves in tedious, repetitive employment, at the same time resenting what they see as the 'spy in the machine', the monitoring facilities made possible by modern microelectronics. And there tends to be a polarisation between the word-processor operators and administrative secretaries who may be freed to do more demanding work.

The deskilling consequences of word processors are not incidental: they are central in the intentions of the equipment designers. Employers obviously have an interest in cost-effective automation that reduces the chances of human error in areas that demand skill or initiative. But equipment provisions of this sort can be counter-productive if staff become demoralised and alienated from their work. It is in the interest of management only to introduce word-processing systems in the context of full discussion with workers and trade unions.

Health

Managements usually introduce word-processing systems with the intention that operators use them for a substantial part of each day. This involves concentration on a visual display unit for lengthy periods, an activity that may have consequences for health. Again, because most word-processor operators are female, such health conditions bear particularly on the situation of women as they come into contact with computer-based systems in the office environment.

It has been pointed out that there are a variety of health hazards in offices (as there are in all working situations): for example, correcting fluids can give off toxic fumes, typists can suffer from backache and neckache, strip lighting can cause problems for epileptics and migraine sufferers, etc. And a word-processor unit or a computer terminal with a display unit (VDU) can bring other problems. A VDU, like a flickery television screen, can cause eyestrain, headaches, fatigue and nausea. It has been suggested that in some circumstances they cause migraine and epileptic fits. The units give off low-level radiation which may be responsible for cataracts. With these possibilities it is clear that the health of women and men in offices equipped with VDUs should be monitored with care.

Concern has been expressed for some time about the potential health hazards involved in sitting in front of a VDU screen for lengthy periods. Reading data on a cathode ray tube screen can cause a variety of physical problems and even psychological reactions, with such consequences particularly likely if the operator already has visual defects — and a third of the UK employee population is reckoned to have uncorrected visual defects. A variety of other factors can increase the likelihood of adverse reactions to VDUs. These include age, general tiredness, anxiety, and the use of drugs, eg the contraceptive pill. The longer one is in contact with a VDU the more intense the effects are likely to be (see, for example, Birnbaum, 1978).

In 1976 Dr G Busch studied the effects of working with VDUs in the American banking and insurance industries. He noted the 'eye strain and visual fatigue created by job tasks performed in a working environment which is ill-suited to healthy work habits,' and added that 'this is particularly true for those work environments utilising visual display units as an important part of the job load.' He isolated what he saw as 'visual fatigue' caused by VDU operation, and listed the following symptoms:

— discomfort of the eye, feeling that eyes are tense, heavy, dry and uncomfortable, burning and tender, producing 'grittiness' (ocular symptoms);

— bad focus, double vision, blurred edges on figures, inability to look in any one direction continuously, colour fringe on objects viewed (visual symptoms);

— headache in forehead with stabbing pains, muscular aches sometimes spreading to the arms and neck areas (systemic symptoms);

— high absentee rates, increase in days lost to illness (behavioural symptoms).

Again the possibility is emphasised that other factors can affect the frequency and intensity of the various symptoms. If the work is boring it may encourage people to consume alcohol or to resort to drugs. Where people are being treated with Valium or Librium, they may be more likely to react adversely to lengthy contact with VDU screens. Alcohol and other drugs make smooth eye movement more difficult, and increase fatigue and eyestrain. The Bird (1980) survey found extensive eyestrain among operators: as many as two thirds of the respondents experienced eyestrain while using new word-processor equipment.

It has been pointed out that VDUs were first used for scientific researchers to turn to occasionally, but 'not to gaze at for eight hours a day' (Pentney, 1981). And it is recognised that ocular symptoms are such things as uncomfortable, heavy, dry eyes which ache, burn, or throb; while problems with focusing, double images or colour fringes indicate eyestrain. Pentney cites research indicating that 10 to 15 per cent of VDU workers have almost daily eye trouble of some sort, with 40 to 50 per cent suffering from time-to-time. Some terminal operators have chosen not to watch television after work.

It was recently reported (*Electronics Weekly*, 25/2/81) that women working at France's biggest national statistical office in Nantes were crippling preparations for the presidential election by refusing to work on computer terminals. Forty female staff began their protest in January. A 22-year old girl was quoted: 'The terminals are turning us into robots. The management refused to give us a 10-minute break each hour, so we began a go-slow. Then the management withheld one day's salary for each working month. That's when we decided to shut down our screens.' Jean-Marie Callies, Director of the Statistical Institute's Nantes centre, locked the keys of the terminals in a safe to prevent the women sabotaging the data banks. (The centre is an important element in the French political and economic system.)

In November 1980 Nixdorf minicomputers were introduced and the women were required to develop a semi-conversational relationship with the terminals. Another woman was quoted: 'On an average day we type between 700 and 1000 pages. When we get tired and letters start dancing in front of our eyes, the only way to stop conversation with the terminal screen is to switch it off. But when we do that we lose our productivity bonus.' We may expect such problems to intensify in circumstances where managements look to productivity without due concern being paid to the needs of their (largely female) word-processor staff.

Some of the complaints about VDU effects may seem unduly alarmist. Pearce (1980) describes recent fears in Norway following the appearance of a face rash among operators. Ten reported cases suggested the possibility of occupational dermatitis, and Tjonn, the medical director at the Directorate of Labour, proposed some form of 'photon sensitivity (?)' as a causal factor (emphasising the use of the question mark). This idea in turn raises the possibility of photo-sensitive epilepsy – about 0.5 per cent of people are epileptic, with about 4 per cent of these being photo-sensitive. Another possibly alarmist incident concerns the birth of four handicapped children in Canada. The mothers had worked on VDUs at a Toronto newspaper during their pregnancies. Initial studies found no excessive X-rays or microwaves radiating from the terminals.

Apart from complaints that may be alarmist there is some suggestion that the adverse effects of VDUs have been exaggerated. The British Optical Information Council (BOIC) finds that recent research has 'tended to confirm the view that working with VDUs presents no more harm to the eyes or the visual ability than watching TV or working with radar screens and the like.' However, concentrated attention on a VDU screen can reveal a previously unsuspected sight defect, and 'working tasks that require specific focusing ability will tend to filter out those that are unsuitable' (*Modern Office and Data Management*, August 1980). The BOIC advises all intending operators to have an eye test before beginning work with VDUs:

This is the common denominator running through all authoritative reports on the effect of VDUs on the health of operators. With these provisos, fears aroused by alarmist reports about radiation and actual eye damage can be allayed.

Concern over the possible effects of VDUs has been sufficient to generate a number of provisions designed to protect operators. These provisions may be considered to fall into two broad (related) categories – *ergonomic* and *trade union.*

The ergonomic suggestions try to define aspects of systems design to achieve maximum human comfort and health in the working environment (see, for example, Appendix 2 in Damodaran et al, 1980). Here there is attention to screen characteristics (character formation, coding format, luminance, etc), keyboard design (key features, keyboard layout, etc), and other features. The aim is to encourage design of equipment (and the equipment environment) to meet human needs, rather than to expect people to cope with equipment however it is designed and configured in the workplace.

Trade union proposals, recognising possible VDU risks, suggest ways of restricting VDU usage to minimise the hazards. For example, some unions (eg TASS, APEX, NALGO and the NUJ) have published recommendations about their use — for instance, that they be used for only 40 minutes in every hour, and for no longer than four hours a day. It has been pointed out that under the Health and Safety at Work Act, unions are legally entitled to elect Safety Representatives who have the right to obtain full details of health and safety factors connected with the introduction of new equipment into the working environment. Typical trade union suggestions, often related to ergonomic considerations, are:

— that offices be properly designed and maintained;

— that there are regular breaks (the TUC recommends a 20-minute break for every two hours of VDU usage;

— that a maximum time allowed in front of the screen should be specified. An agreement between the CPSA and the Post Office specifies 100 minutes maximum per day, with no operator to work more than 50 minutes without a proper break (gaps in the workflow do not count);

— that regular medical and eye check-ups be carried out, with realistic compensation agreed for eye damage, and guaranteed other jobs to move to.

APEX (the Association of Professional, Executive, Clerical and Computer Staffs), for example, has proposed health and safety provisions for VDU usage. These suggest such things as pre-employment eye testing, agreements that certain vulnerable employees (eg those suffering from persistent stress headaches, migraines, epilepsy, nervous complaints) not be required to operate VDUs, that contact with the VDU be limited to 40 minutes in every hour, etc. APEX has negotiated such provisions with various organisations, including International Harvester, Coventry Climax, and (in conjunction with ASTMS) British Airways. Similarly, an ASTMS guide suggests a range of ergonomic and health provisions for use of VDU equipment (see bibliography).

The traditional 'shunting' of women into typist and secretarial positions has meant that the new word-processing equipment is largely operated by women: it is an obvious step for management to train a typist to operate a word processor. Men obviously also use VDUs in the office and other working environments, but they are less likely to focus on a screen hour after hour, every day of the working week. In contrast, it is the *intention* of word-processor manufacturers and company managements that word-processor operators — mainly women — be so employed. For this reason, the health considerations concerning prolonged VDU usage bear main-ly on women, rather than men, in the office environment.

SUMMARY

Where women come into contact with computer-based systems in offices, the overall situation has many of the elements we have observed in other areas of computing. Women are expected (eg as word-processor operators) to perform the straightforward and routine tasks — an aim of word-processor design and manufacture is to make jobs less, rather than more, skilled. The more skilled work associated with word processors (eg where separate keys pro-vide a sophisticated data processing capability) is more likely to be performed by a man 'while the girl is handling the post.' There is evidence also of the familiar 'tokenism', whereby a few women are upgraded into 'administrative secretaries' or 'word-processor super-visors' but only rarely into senior managers in the organisation.

Many of the advantages of word-processing systems and other computer-based systems in offices are consistent with any 'social structure'. There is nothing inherent in automation that necessar-ily implies increased discrimination, the shunting of women into low-grade activity, alienation from work, etc. It is perfectly poss-ible, theoretically, for women and men to share necessary office drudgery, to have similar (limited) contact with computer-based systems that might represent a health hazard, etc. Where discrimin-atory or exploitative patterns exist in the office environment, they generally reflect aspects of the broader culture. Offices are part of society: we should not be surprised that they exhibit the same 'social patterns' that we have observed in other areas using computer-based systems.

5 Freelance and Home-Based Work

INTRODUCTION

The most obvious constraint on women developing a career is the likelihood of their taking on competing domestic commitments. Marriage may not be a handicap in this respect, though a large number of successful career women — in data processing and elsewhere — are single or divorced. Childbirth, and the ensuing dependency of offspring in the early years, are likely to interrupt a woman's career development, even if she is professionally well qualified and able to operate in a non-discriminatory environment. (We cannot consider here the desirability of baby- or child-care facilities. For our purposes we must look at prevailing social and industrial circumstances.)

For many women, it is ideal to be able to combine domestic activities and professional work. In the computer industry, contract programming can lend itself to this sort of arrangement. For more than two decades, experienced female programmers have been employed in their own homes, sometimes doing all the required work in that environment and sometimes visiting on-site installations when necessary. This chapter outlines the circumstances of freelance and part-time working in the data processing industry, and briefly profiles some of the people and companies active in this field. (As with the profiles in earlier chapters, in no sense does Chapter 5 aim to provide a comprehensive Who's Who or an exhaustive guide to companies offering freelance or part-time programming work.)

HOME-BASED WORK

The shortage of experienced computer staff in the UK and other countries encourages companies to look at the possibility of employing freelance and part-time workers. In one estimate (see *Freelance*, 1980) there was a UK shortage of specialist data processing staff amounting to 25,000, attributed in part to how the 1971 slump affected training. Through the 1970s more and more companies were acquiring computer equipment while the central pool of specialist staff was scarcely increasing. Companies clearly have an interest in seeking out appropriate trained staff wherever it exists — and, where women are concerned, this is often in the home.

Some data processing managers are reluctant to use contract staff, thinking that it may be difficult to control their activities when they work at home. Other managers recognise that a freelance pool of specialist staff can be useful in many ways: people can be called in on specific projects to which they are well suited, they can be used to train permanent staff, to help relieve staff shortages, and to cope with fluctuations in workload. Though it may not be cheap to use a contract programmer, this approach may make economic sense for particular short-run projects. And employers may feel confident in employing freelance staff from contract agencies who belong to the Computer Services Association (CSA), eg F International Ltd (see below).

There are various classes of people who may wish to offer programming services from a home base. The disabled, people with dependent relatives, or those (usually women) who have domestic commitments to young children may be highly qualified but less mobile than people in situations different to their own. A variety of companies have exploited the fact that there are many people who work on a regular basis inside the home. This particularly applies to women with obvious family commitments. It tends to be assumed, rightly or wrongly, that if babies or young children have to be looked after at home it will be the mother, rather than the father, who is expected to take on this role.

Efforts have been made for many years to recruit home-based female programmers. Freelance Programmers Ltd, out of which the F International Group was to grow, was founded in 1962, and around that time efforts were being made by various companies to build up panels of experienced female programmers working from a home base. By 1970, GEC-Elliott Software Limited, launched by GEC-Elliott Automation, was recruiting women as home-based programmers (see Woollcombe, 1970). The aim at that time was to link women working ,at home to two Marconi-Elliott computers at Watford. Freelance Programmers Ltd had, in 1970, some 250 staff — almost all women including 175 analysts, programmers and consultants.

A (1970) spokesman for the GEC-Elliott Computer Software Company claimed that the firm had really initiated a 'cottage industry'. The idea was to install remote data terminals in the women's homes, on-line to the Watford computer centre, to provide software services to other companies within the group and later to other computer manufacturers. At that time it was apparent that freelance programming was expanding in various companies outside the UK. (We have already seen* that a large proportion of the early US programmers were women. It was sensible of US firms to use the skills of experienced female programmers who may have left the industry to start families.)

By the late-1970s a number of companies in the US and elsewhere had become well established as freelance programmer agencies (see below). And there were a variety of other experiments with home-based working. In one article (Clutterbuck, 1979 i) the activities of two home-based employees of the US Continental Illinois Corporation are profiled. Both of the home operators were already established members of the company when they were offered the chance to participate in a home-based experiment in using word processors. One of the operators, but not the other, had already worked with a word processor. Both women took to the new arrangements with confidence and enthusiasm.

Initially there were system breakdowns, and the method of transmitting tapes to the operators' homes had to be changed several times. At one time, an operator at headquarters had to repeat the tapes aloud over the telephone. There were also problems with people who were poor at dictation because the home operators

* Chapter 2

were unable to talk to them personally to sort out problems. (One manager dictated at home whilst watching a televised sports programme. Background noise caused confusion, and every time his team came close to scoring, 'the manager completely lost his thread of thought.')

By July 1979 the home operators had greatly improved their productivity (90 lines an hour, compared with 106 lines an hour from typists in the headquarters buildings). The home operators were obliged to wait while tapes were transmitted to their own dictaphones and in transmitting completed work back to the computer. System improvements to facilitate equal productivity were envisaged. It was thought that up to 70 per cent of the typing work in the company's trust department could in due course be put out to home operators (according to Jean Allen, manager of staff services). Clutterbuck (1979 i) outlines the advantages of the new arrangements to both the company and the two word-processor operators.

Such an arrangement allows a company to choose its typing staff from a much wider range of people. Furthermore, there are cost savings in office space, associated overheads, and fringe benefits. The system allows for greater flexibility than a company may expect with permanent employment. Home operators can organise their activities to cope with periods of heavy workload, and if there is a sudden domestic pressure the operator can choose to work late in the evening on company business.

Flexibility of this sort for home-based word-processor operators and contract programmers can be valuable to both companies and staff. Often such facilities are linked to part-time working. For example, Lucas Industries (UK) and Jonas Oglaend (Norway) have introduced short shifts of four or five hours. These have been dubbed *housewives'* or *mothers'* shifts. The organisation training director of Oglaend notes that 'the housewives can pick and choose which shift they wish to work and which best fits in with their domestic needs.' Early evening shifts have been popular with housewives and employers.

GEC Measurement Ltd (UK) take on women to work early-evening ('twilight') shifts on contracts lasting between six and 13 weeks. Hodgkinson, general manager: 'Our full-time workforce is geared to meet only our minimum production requirements and the part-timers take care of temporary increases. This enables us to provide greater job security to our workforce and we avoid having to lay off people' (quoted by Clutterbuck, 1979 ii). The French government has observed that 'employers more and more will have to take into account the family obligations of working women, particularly mothers and those seeking careers.' In 1979 the French ministries of health and employment began giving Wednesdays off to women employees with children under the age of sixteen. This is part of an experiment by government before such provisions are imposed by law. And the West German Federation of Employers Associations has exerted pressure on member firms to create more part-time jobs for women as well as for older workers. It has recommended that companies take into account school hours and public-transport time-tables when designing jobs for housewives.

A Swedish survey showed that two-thirds of unemployed housewives would like to start a job, preferably part-time with convenient hours and near to their homes. And in Holland there are special provisions for married women: for example, unemployed people seeking only part-time work are entitled to receive unemployment benefits – this arrangement is particularly relevant to the situation of women with young children. In France it has been observed that nearly half of all women seeking employment have children.

Provisions for flexible and part-time working are relevant to data processing, as they are to all other areas of industry. Micro Switch (a Honeywell division), for example, has tackled a number of personnel problems by hiring part-time workers. The personnel manager Louise Hale observed: 'We were having great difficulty finding dependable beginners. They had no interest in their jobs. They were constantly bored. They were unproductive ...' When she placed a single advertisement in a local newspaper, aimed at house-bound wives, more than a hundred women applied for twenty vacancies.

Micro Switch has adopted a flexible policy towards part-timers, but requires that they work at least four hours and not more than six in a day. Once the hours are agreed they can only be changed

when absolutely necessary (Hale: 'Otherwise it would be very difficult for our supervisors'). During the period of the summer school
holidays, the company hires college students to replace the women
who look after their children at home.

The data processing industry needs to exploit all the available
trained staff, including house-bound women who have programming and other computer-oriented skills. US companies are experi-
menting with recruitment policies. For example, the Wells Fargo
Bank in California has 35 disabled staff — blind, mentally retarded,
deaf, autistic, etc — in its data processing operations (other employees are taking sign-language classes). The position of the disabled has been likened to that of women, in that there is discrimination against both groups for reason of prejudice and misinform-
ation.

Increasingly it is being recognised that there is a substantial
body of talent represented by house-bound people (mainly wom-
en) skilled in programming and other fields of computing. It
should be obvious to companies that various schemes — working at
home, working part-time on site, working flexible hours, etc — can
be introduced to tap this valuable reservoir of ability.

We should not be surprised that a housewife might want to
work only those hours when her children are at school, or that she
may wish to work, though unable to leave the house at all because
of a young baby or a dependent ageing relative. The provision of a
computer terminal in her home can answer many of the obvious
mobility problems. A number of companies, in Europe and the
US, have discovered that this is an effective way of allowing skilled
house-bound women (and, less frequently, men) to pursue a career
and to meet domestic obligations. This sort of arrangement is of
benefit both to the individuals concerned and to the employers. It
is worth profiling some of the (mainly UK) companies that have
adopted this approach as a central element in their operating phil-
osophy.

F INTERNATIONAL GROUP

Freelance Programmers Ltd (fpl), the forerunner to the F International Group, was formed in 1962 by Mrs Stephanie ('Steve')
Shirley. She set up the company, when forced to leave work

because of pregnancy, to provide clients with a wide range of scientific and commercial data processing applications: programming, program specifications, planning and techniques, program maintenance and audits. A main aim was 'to utilise, wherever practicable, the services of people with domestic responsibilities or who are otherwise unable to work in a conventional office mode.'

F2 was the data processing and systems consultancy that evolved from the systems division of fpl. More than 50 staff were employed to work on feasibility studies, hardware and software evaluation, systems analysis and design, and consultancy. Systems designed by F2 were frequently implemented by fpl, providing full continuity of both project management and staff. F2 and fpl together formed one of the country's largest software houses, F International. There are now two subsidiary companies – F International ApS in Copenhagen, serving Scandinavia, and F International BV in Amsterdam, serving the Benelux countries.

The staff of F International consists mainly of a panel of highly skilled data processing practitioners, coordinating into teams according to their experience. Team leaders act as links between the company and the staff in their areas of interest, providing the flow of necessary technical information, allocating budgets, and exercising complete control over each project. This allows the consultancy to deploy a wide range of skills. F International panel members – with experience in commerce, industry and administration – are drawn from accountancy, engineering, insurance, computing, research and management. Exacting standards of procedure and documentation are seen as a support to the creativity of the systems effort.

F International, with administrative headquarters in Chesham (Bucks), now employs more than 600 staff, mostly women. In the UK the company operates in four regions with regional managers responsible for all work from initial proposal to implementation and acceptance. Since much of the work is being undertaken remotely, project control is essential for proper estimating, the maintenance of staff performance records, and regular auditing. F International has many clients, including AERE (Harwell), the AA, British Gas, ICL, Lloyds Bank, the Open University, Unilever, Volkswagen (GB), and the Yorkshire Regional Health Authority.

Of the 600 technical and non-technical staff employed in the UK, the majority are women with young children. There are also some disabled people, and people looking after elderly dependants. The women employed by F International usually aim to work for the company for between 20 and 25 hours a week, combining home commitments with an active career. Most of the working time is spent at home with visits made to clients' offices for discussions, reviews, and computer testing. A number of the home-based programmers have terminals which can be linked to a computer via the Post Office telephone line.

Few women reach management status before they start a family, and so the company develops staff potential within the organisation. Training is provided in management techniques, including resources planning and control, finance, staff supervision, and development. F International, being independent of any manufacturer, can also advise on the purchase of computer hardware. The staff average more than ten years' experience each, and staff continuity in the company is unusually high for the industry. Secretaries, like the programmers, also work from their home base.

Mrs Steve Shirley left her job as a senior computer programmer in the sixties to set up on her own as a 'systems house', employing women part-time in their own homes. At that time this was a quite new arrangement — an all-woman computing venture and a novel concept in business organisation. By 1981 the company could claim a million-pound order, a large number of satisfied clients, and an annual turnover of around £3 million. (Shirley: 'Usually we have a queue of people waiting to join us. I like to think that what we have to offer is not only a job, but career progression. Employees move up to become executives, managers of various departments, or consultants.')

Many of the F International staff have been with the company for more than ten years. Suzette Harold, for example, now managing director, has been profiled in various journals (eg *Datamation*, August 1976; *Computer Talk*, 14/3/79). In 1974 and 1975, Harold stood for election to Parliament twice, had two children, and took over as F International's managing director.

In the early sixties she had worked for various atomic energy establishments, mainly in the Oxford area. When an Atlas computer system was installed in the Chiltern laboratory, she was concerned with information retrieval projects. Her first project for F International was a critical path program for the Atomic Energy Research Establishment at Harwell, involving work on IBM 360/65 and 360/75 computers. Then, with other people, she was involved in automating a British standard ('Towards the end of the project I was asked to take a management role'). By 1968 Harold was firmly established in management, and in 1970 became production manager, controlling the growing number of autonomous project managers. In 1975 she became Steve Shirley's deputy for a few months, before being officially appointed as director in November. Today she is involved with various committees, such as the local branch of the Institute of Data Processing Management, the British Institute of Management, and a committee for the Institute of Directors.

Another long-standing F International employee is Penny Tutt, who joined the company in 1969 and is now the firm's company secretary ('The company... provides facilities for developing management potential within the firm, so there are just as many chances for promotion as in a conventionally organised business... We aren't a band of militant women, intent upon changing the fabric of society. We go into a job as professional people, not as women. We are just a group of women who enjoy working but also enjoy being wives and mothers. In that respect we're one step ahead of the women's libbers, because we have made the best of both worlds' – quoted in *Computer Weekly*, 8/11/79). Tutt has a background in social services, banking and civil aviation. As a director of F International BV, the Benelux subsidiary, she makes regular working visits to Europe.

Other senior F International staff include Brenda Chapman, Northern regional manager (joined in 1970 as a systems analyst); Jean Fox, senior systems consultant (joined in 1963 and has been responsible for many commercial and scientific assignments); Ursula Buesst, central regional manager (joined in 1968 with a background in operational research and commercial data processing); Janet Lennon, Western regional manager (joined in 1978, with previous responsibility at Leyland International for seventeen overseas installations); and Diane Taylor, manager of the estimating department (joined in 1974 with ten years' experience of programming and consultancy).

The innovatory character of F International has made it inevitable that its staff should attract media attention. Steve Shirley herself, apart from being profiled in the technical and general press, has spoken on radio and appeared in BBC and ITV programmes. She has also made two short films for the Central Office of Information. Other F International personnel, as we have seen, have been interviewed for journals and newspapers.

Angela Ginger, economics graduate and senior computer system analyst became an area manager for F International (*Manchester Evening News*, 15/5/79). By 1979 she had 100 women on her books and was responsible for an area bounded by the Potteries, the Pennines and Cumbria. The task of an area manager is to find employment for the women on her books, to schedule the work, and to monitor progress ('The work has given me financial security and makes me feel like a person in my own right, not just someone's wife and mother. But I don't consider myself to be a feminist — I'm just one of the lucky ones who has the best of both worlds. I still like to have people open doors for me'.)

Teresa Sheiham, an F International employee, does work that includes systems analysis, quoting for the company's estimating department, programming, technical coordination of projects, and the auditing of programs (*Computer Weekly*, 15/11/79). She has worked on warehouse pre-planning, marketing systems, pension systems, insurance, and project control ('I enjoy the variety of clients and type of work. High standards set by the company make people unusually conscientious and highly self-motivated').

Sue Crorie is another freelance computer programmer on F International's books (*Glasgow Herald*, 5/2/80). She works at home, in a tiny village just south of Crieff, and then visits a client's site to test out equipment ('If it was not for the existence of F International I would simply be a housewife at home all day looking after a toddler'). Crorie's experience is similar to that of hundreds of other women in the UK who — via F International and a few other companies — have managed to combine highly-skilled professional home-based work with demanding domestic commitments.

HEIGHTS INC

In 1979, Heights Information Technology Service Inc opened offices in Oakland (Calif) and White Plains (NY) with the aim of offering projects on a contract basis to programmers and systems analysts. Heights is building up a large panel of experienced home-based computer specialists. The new company, ideal for the working mother, is also intended to cater for any other type of individual who has a good reason for wanting to work at home. This can include single fathers and handicapped individuals.

Heights patterned itself after, and is affiliated with, F International. In 1978 Luanne James, Heights adviser and co-founder, met Anne Russell, one of the founders of F International, and brought the relevant ideas back to the US. F International offered management support and advice, and training in the use of special techniques that have been developed for project specification, estimating, scheduling and control. Heights has negotiated a contract to use F International's name and techniques in the US.

By 1980 Heights had handled about 90 contracts from the two original offices, and had established a developing panel of professional staff. The company requires at least three years of work experience from prospective programmers and at least five years' experience from its systems analysts. It is observed that though women may face less discrimination in data processing than in many other professions, they still have to fight against the idea that their career is over once they have left the workforce to have a baby (James: 'It's difficult not to work full-time and continue in career pathing'). It is also emphasised that although the bulk of Heights panel members (about 30 in early-1980) are women, men are not excluded. One of the early panel members was a man, a father who wanted to look after his children at home while his wife attended college.

Heights also runs a nontechnical panel of typists ('We work on a project structure. Each contract we get is assigned to a project manager for coordination and he or she, if it is wished, can hire a typist from his or her own neighbourhood'). To date, Heights' biggest project has taken five people six months to complete (compared with an F International project involving 48 people for two years).

James sees Heights eventually using a time-sharing network whereby two or more offices could work together on a job with wide geographical spread. Two central principles are recognised — that there are many house-bound people with special computing skills, and that there is a substantial shortage of qualified programmers and systems analysts in the data processing industry (James: 'This shortage of qualified people combined with the expanding need for such activities will generate a considerable growth of business activity.')

Again, Heights — like F International in the UK and elsewhere — is enabling home-based specialists, mainly women, to combine a career and domestic responsibilities. It is an obviously successful strategy for ambitious women who nonetheless wish to stay at home with babies or young children.

PAMELA WOODMAN ASSOCIATES

This company (PWA, Software Services International) is another organisation dedicated to the effective employment of home-based women. Pamela Woodman: '... our organisation is particularly geared towards the effective utilisation of women who, on leaving full-time employment in the computer industry, seek a second career in computing which will combine well with family life.'

PWA was founded in 1972 by Pamela Woodman to provide software services to government, industry and commerce. With headquarters in Cupar, Fife, the company operates throughout the UK, serving clients in almost every major field. PWA has also contributed to various important government projects.

Pamela Woodman, the founder and managing director, began her career in 1954 as a machine operator with the Commercial Union Assurance Group (CU). In 1956 she was promoted to manager of the hollerith machine room at Exeter, and in 1960 was invited to join the first CU computer planning group in London. After working for NCR (as senior programmer), English Electric (as a consultant) and Unilever (as a systems manager), she joined Freelance Programmers Ltd (now F International) where, over a period of seven years, she held various managerial positions. In 1971 she became managing director.

Today Pamela Woodman gives as her reasons for running PWA:

- To create opportunities for computer professionals to work on a part-time basis, should this be necessary for domestic or other reasons;

- To provide commerce and industry in the UK with a first-class consultancy and software service;

- To use my own skills as a manager to benefit other people;

- To provide myself with an income.

In the main, women have been appointed to the senior executive positions within the company. At the systems/programming level the staff are freelance (90 per cent women, 10 per cent men), with about 100 consultants on the PWA register. Pamela Woodman has pointed out that there is an ample supply of part-time programmers, mainly married women, 'usually very skilled indeed' and able to 'perform very well provided that they are managed effectively and given clear objectives.' Again it is noted that part-time programming is well suited to mothers, as the work can be carefully defined and can be performed at flexible times during the day.

Most of the programming takes place at home, with program testing carried out either on the client's premises or via portable terminals at home. Some of the senior PWA programmers, who may need to leave their homes for a substantial part of the day, employ babysitters to resolve the mobility problem. At one time, PWA considered setting up a creche at the office but abandoned the idea as the programmers are located in such diverse areas. (One of the PWA clients has installed a full creche service for female employees with children. Each mother pays from her salary a contribution towards the overheads and also spends a certain amount of her time in the creche each week.)

The use of terminals in the home can assist program testing and relieve the mobility problem. However, PWA has found such devices to be expensive in terms of computer time and only cost-effective if reserved for senior programmers. The majority of the analysts are female with children of school age. The women work an average of 24 hours per week with 18 spent on site, with the rest of the work (reporting-writing, minutes of meetings, etc) being conducted at home.

PWA are experiencing a shortfall of staff in the areas of project and line management. To date the company has always appointed female project managers on a full- or part-time basis. Where a project manager is a married woman, it is recognised that an organised home and a husband who is sympathetic to his wife's career are prerequisites to the success of the venture. Pamela Woodman: 'During my 15 years involvement with the employment of women on a part-time basis I have worked with some women who have successfully combined a senior management role with their family lives over a long-term period.' At the same time it is recognised that there are problems ('I do not believe this type of work is generally suited to mothers of young children unless of course they are in the position to, and wish to, have their offspring cared for by a nanny, a childminder or other third party').

Future expansion will depend upon the number of senior staff, probably women, available to perform key functions. Key PWA staff today include Janet Broom (senior project manager) and Margaret Martin, quotations manager. Mrs Broom began her computing career with ICL in 1967 where, after training in commercial programming, she was assigned to a team involved in developing a system for the Post Office. In 1971 she joined Datasolve International, prior to joining PWA in 1973, to be appointed, four years later, project manager. Mrs Martin worked first at Teddington Admiralty Research Laboratory, and later at Ferranti/ICL, writing programs and lecturing. After working at a software house, she joined PWA in 1972, taking over responsibility for the quotations department in 1978.

PWA has demonstrated, like F International, that women can combine a skilled professional career and domestic commitments; and that women can make highly competent managers in the computer industry.

ROBERT SHERRY & ASSOCIATES

This company (based in Chorley, Lancashire) has been established for about ten years. In its early years it concentrated mainly on systems development work. In 1978 it began employing home-based staff, mainly women, to carry out program development and other tasks. An aim is to provide specialist people, confined to the home environment, with appropriate work. There is currently a panel of about 20 programmers, the vast majority being married women with domestic responsibilities.

All the programmers on the panel are highly qualified. All have at least four years' programming experience — and some over ten. Most can offer at least two programming languages and the organisation has programmers with knowledge of most computers in common use.

The company has found that many home-based programmers have difficulty in making frequent visits to installations. For this reason, efforts are made to find programming projects that can be scheduled on a completely off-site basis. This organisation is currently interested in the possibility of carrying out home-based software development for microcomputers. The company offers a variety of services:

- Systems development on- or off-site. Systems development off-site is generally carried out using terminals linked to either customer machines or to the bureau services to which the company subscribes, or on microcomputers which it owns or leases. Use is made of bureau facilities which provide a 24-hour service and fully interactive development facilities;

- Microcomputer software package development;

- Contract programming on-site;

- Contract systems maintenance off-site, using terminals linked to customer machines;

- Consultancy services (eg MAPCON feasibility studies).

ICL CONTRACT PROGRAMMING

In 1970 ICL formed Contract Programming Services, part of the Southern Development Division, to keep trained staff active in programming who would otherwise have been lost when they left to have children (its founder noted that the scheme was an instance of 'flexitime gone mad'). CPS is run by home-based staff, mainly women, working between 16 and 30 hours per week on a variety of projects that can be carried out off-site (mainly software and systems maintenance, with some development and technical writing). CPS staff in due course achieved management responsibility for a number of projects, including maintenance of the System 4.

Hilary Cropper, the woman behind the organisation and a former ICL programmer, acknowledges committed ICL management support: 'The company management's dedication to make it work is a major reason for its success.' In the early stages there were credibility problems but by 1977, 'we are over the credibility gap and people are seeing our results.' Today CPS staff expertise covers all ICL equipment and represents an average computing experience of ten years per person.

No-one with less than three years' experience in the industry is considered for CPS – partly because it is difficult to train home-based people. Around 90 per cent of CPS staff are former full-time ICL employees. At the same time there are difficulties. Cropper: 'There are vast numbers of women who are dying for work at home, but so few people give out decent work at home that the opportunities are limited.'

Some women leave CPS to have children, and then return. And others do not have a family but prefer home-based employment. For example, Marilyn Scattergood used CPS to combine an interest in technical writing and programming experience. Formerly an ICT technical writer (and later in ICL sales), she joined CPS in 1974, developing her career to run the CPS team with responsibility for customer literature for 1900, System 4 and 2903 computers.

Within CPS there has been a growing demand for management expertise. Increasingly there has been a requirement for the organisation to handle complete projects, thus necessitating adequate management structures. There has been progressive CPS development into new ICL areas: for example, into commercial program development for various sales regions.

SUMMARY

There is a sense in which freelance, home-based work for women represents an alternative strategy to that proposed by mainstream feminist organisations. Freelance work is usually part-time: it typically requires that a person work about twenty hours a week. It tends to be predicated on the assumption that many women do not wish to give up minding their own babies or looking after their own small children. It is an effort to unite career ambitions and domestic responsibilities.

There is no doubt that contract programming — as organised by the relatively small number of companies in this area — has brought immense benefits to hundreds of women. This mode of working could serve as a model for home-based employment in other industry sectors.

6 The Future

INTRODUCTION

There are problems in predicting the future, but the problems vary from one field to another. The predictions about which we are most confident — eg concerning tides or eclipses — tend to be, in some sense, trivial. They give us few insights into human potential or the stability of societies. We are less confident about social predictions: the variables are too uncertain and too numerous to be subsumed in a nicely formal mathematics. Any predictions about the position of women in society — or in the data processing industry in particular — are bound to have a tentative and partial flavour.

Some emerging disciplines, linked closely to theories of probability and social dynamics, try to organise the predictive task on a formal basis. Distinctions are made between 'sufficient' and 'necessary' conditions for social change, and efforts are made to scrutinise past predictions to see why they were in error. In 'retrospective futurology', for example, data may be scrutinised for a year in the past and then predictions attempted for a more recent year. When the predictions are complete, the known data for the more recent year is compared with the predictions. Ideally the two are the same. Discrepancies can be used to refine technique and, hopefully, to make subsequent predictions more accurate.

There is always a 'conditional' element in prediction; ie assuming *this*, then *such-and-such* will be the case. With social and political issues, areas where human volition is taken to be highly important, the conditional element is central. In our context, the women's position in data processing will be such-and-such, only if certain measures are taken by government and managements, and certain attitudes adopted by women and men.

CONDITIONS FOR CHANGE

If we take as a factual premise that discrimination against women can be shown to exist in the data processing industry, and as an ethical premise that discrimination is wrong, we are then entitled to look at the social provisions that are necessary for improvements to take place.

An initial requirement is that society survive broad threats to its continued existence. Nuclear war would do little for women's rights in the UK or elsewhere. Another required condition is that broad conditions of national economic stability prevail. We have seen that economic recession tends to hit women harder than men — partly because it is easier to dispense with low-grade labour, and partly because (male) fears of unemployment fuel traditional prejudices. It is hard to be liberal, ie conscious of others' rights, at a time you are being made redundant.

Governments can help to establish the appropriate progressive framework by legislation. To the extent that there are relatively new anti-discrimination laws on the statute in many countries, there have been significant progressive gains in recent years. At the same time, much of the prevailing legislation leaves loopholes or is not pressed with sufficient vigour. Such circumstances relate to how keenly managers and other individuals feel the injustice of discrimination, ie how effectively the 'spirit' of the legislation informs the actual laws.

There are 'nebulous' factors that determine the impact of any just (or unjust) legislation. If large sections of a population are unsympathetic to a law, it is unlikely to be fully effective. And prejudice has a seductive power: it can, in the total absence of reason, strongly influence attitudes and behaviour.

STEPS TO TAKE

There is a self-sustaining circle of discrimination that has a constant, negative impact on the position of women in computing. In schools it is often assumed that girls will not pursue a career that involves science or mathematics. Two fifth-form girls, taking physics on their own 'in a desert of boys', have been quoted: 'They say that men are better than girls, and girls shouldn't be doing physics. Physics is really a boys' subject. And they'd say this straight to our faces.' Such attitudes can be difficult to cope with, particularly at a time when girls are eager for male approval. Research has shown that girls taking science tend not to think of themselves as popular or attractive (see *The Missing Half, Girls and Science Education*, Manchester University Press).

An inevitable consequence of this situation is that relatively few women become scientists or technicians — thus providing a bogus confirmation that women are ill-suited to such occupations. There are relatively few women computer specialists, thus 'proving' that women are better employed elsewhere.

Efforts should be made to break the circle at various points.* Governments should tidy up existing anti-discrimination legislation, and give stronger teeth to monitoring organisations such as the Equal Opportunities Commission (EOC). School programmes should be organised so that there are no pressures to stereotype male and female subjects and subsequent career paths. And company managements should be sensitive to the special need for positive policies to advance the position of employed women. (Some of the possible schemes have been explored in the present book.) Manufacturers and other employers should consider flexible attitudes to employment for the benefit of those women (and men) wishing to combine career advancement and domestic commitments. F International and a few other companies have pioneered methods of exploiting — to great success — the specialist abilities of home-based personnel.

SUMMARY

A more just, and more rational, pattern for female and male employment in the computer industry is possible — granted certain social and company provisions. In the Third World, where claims even for the most basic human rights may be seen as sedit-

* See also Steps to Take (Chapter 3).

ious, radical measures may be necessary, and these cannot be divorced from broader political questions. In the developed world, there is nothing within the institutional fabric of different nations that should discourage people from working for reform. There is broad supportive legislation and a high level of anti-discrimination consciousness.

The future is mediated by a host of social and economic factors, and few of these are independent of human decision-making, human attitudes, and human behaviour. Economic recession causes problems in the field of human rights, as it does in other areas. But the cyclic nature of trade dynamics suggests that, sooner or later, we will emerge from depressed national economies and have new social and industrial opportunities. One of these will be the enhanced opportunity to give legitimate scope to female career expectations in the modern world. Apart from being socially just, this approach makes good economic sense. Sensible managements are unlikely to neglect indefinitely the human resources that reside in half the human race.

Appendix 1

Case Studies

I interviewed eleven women at Dataskil. They were chosen to reflect a diversity of job titles: by chance, variations in age, background and years of work experience also emerged. To some extent, awareness of, and attitudes towards, sex discrimination seem related to these varying factors. For example, the younger women tend to be less aware of sex discrimination, especially of the implicit type, than do older women, who are apparently more sensitive to overt and implicit discriminatory behaviour.

The five case studies in this appendix are representative of the general parameters outlined above.

Pamela Poe

INTRODUCTION

Institutional sexism exists. It is to be found in Dataskil and count-less other male-dominated companies. Legislation does not change the man's expectation that the only woman in the office is the secr-etary. Discriminatory attitudes characterise most men, and male managers are far from being exceptions to the rule. Men are likely to be baffled when a super-qualified consultant, hired to improve a company's profitability, turns out to be a woman.

Anti-discrimination legislation certainly cannot be expected to change attitudes overnight. In the experiences of the Dataskil women, the law seems to have had little effect even on behaviour. The Dataskil men about whom I heard seem unaware of their im-plicitly discriminatory behaviour. (A Dataskil woman applying for a a line-management position was asked 'If you got this job wouldn't your husband be ever so upset if his tea is not on the table when he gets home?')

Even women can be unaware of existing discriminatory attitudes. (Although another Dataskil woman says she has never suffered sex discrimination she notes 'If I had been a boy I think they would have taken greater consideration about my choice of 'O' levels'.) There is a need for 'consciousness raising' in both sexes of all ages. There is a need for women 'who have made it' to nurture those who hope to. And women in computing have begun various 'net-working' organisations to do just that. There is a need for women to have female manager role models.

There are various duties and responsibilities in this situation. Parents, for example, could demand that the schools provide knowledgeable and non-sexist counselling — which would help to prevent girls being channelled into the arts, and boys into the sciences; and subsequently women into teaching and men into engineering; or mummy at home with children, and daddy at work making a fool of himself by mistaking that £30,000-a-year female consultant for the copy-machine operator. And parents should also take some responsibility for a proper 'values education' of their children, so that sex discrimination is encouraged to go the way of the ENIAC computer.

More enlightening early life experiences will spawn a generation of managers who assess their colleagues according to their abilities, skills and performance rather than assuming social limitations attached to sex roles. Perhaps we can look forward to a climate where the situation that Jane of Dataskil describes ('You do sometimes have to work harder to prove you do know') is a thing of the past.

SUZANNE

Suzanne is a 24-year-old senior programmer whose father is an engineer and mother a teacher. Although she spent some time in school abroad in her parents' native country, she attended a girls' school in England from the age of eleven.

'I think I was very lucky. Because we were all girls somebody had to do science so it was never split – boys do science and girls do arts,' Suzanne notes. She did what she describes as 'a weird combination of 'O' levels – 3 maths, history and English'. Although they wanted her to stay on to do Oxbridge, Suzanne said she had 'had enough by then' and decided to do maths at London. The college she attended was about 90% male – which she thought was very restrictive for the men.

For six months after receiving her degree, Suzanne did accountancy but found it 'incredibly boring' and decided she would never be among the 17% who qualify. As her husband was doing computing and enjoying it and as she quite liked her computing experience at university, she joined Dataskil, where she has received her only real training. In two years she's learned PLAN and four mainframes.

Suzanne would like job advancement but only on the technical side to team leader. At her initial interview she asked the man who was to become her manager, how many female team leaders there were in Dataskil. When asked why she had made that enquiry, Suzanne answered 'because sex discrimination does exist,' but says she feels very lucky because she has never experienced it. But is it just luck? Suzanne conjectures, 'I think it has to do with my education. They don't really care... whether you are male or female. As long as you have the right qualifications – that's been my experience anyway.'

Getting back to management, Suzanne thinks effective managers must know the people on the team, choose the right people for the jobs, and give them space to meet deadlines. She says a manager must have the ability to support his decisions and learn to live with having his work interrupted by members of the team.

When asked if men seem rather more apt than women to exhibit those kinds of behaviour Suzanne answered, 'I don't think I can say because the only managers I've had have been men.' She went on to say that women's early training might be limiting, 'they just aren't given their head in the beginning.' Of her own early years she says, 'I just happen to be lucky that my parents were reasonably modern and they just didn't think girls should be conditioned one way or the other.'

Another woman on the team has been there for what Suzanne calls a long while, and she's helped, explained and sorted-out for Suzanne, '...problems... things you just don't understand about computing.' But the men have helped, too and she says, '...It's very nice getting into a team.'

Suzanne's advice to young women wanting a career in computing is to acquire some sort of science background. Why? She answers, 'Things like a semi-colon are important in coding. Some sort of scientific logical training would be a help I think.'

JULIA

'It wasn't a matter of career counselling. I had decided for myself that I wanted to go into computing,' said Julia, a 27-year-old-project leader who has been with Dataskil for six years.

Julia's interest in computers began in the lower sixth when instead of doing 'A' level maths, she took a course in Fortran from a teacher who had herself just taken a crash course. The programs were sent off to the county council computer and even with a two-week turn-round, Julia's interest continued because 'It was something nice and logical and my mind agreed with it.'

The product of a little village primary school and a girls' high school, Julia identified early-on her ability to enjoy maths and pursued that course of study. She says 'You know career counselling; if you've got an idea and they can't see anything against it, they are not going to try to push you into anything else.'

Realising her ability at maths, picking up the teacher on flow charts that were not as efficient as they could be, knowing she did not want to teach and being expected to go to university so as not to waste the high school space Julia observes, 'There wasn't a terrific amount left that I saw really available.'

A course of maths and computer science at university saw Julia in a situation where one student in four was a woman. She remembers no limitations or adverse situations from that ratio − except that the men were easily manipulated to do the jobs the women did not relish.

'There are the brochures, go and have a look − and then you got on with it yourself, really,' is how Julia remembers being advised about the world of work. She does not remember if there was advice about which companies had vacancies, but she got an offer from Dataskil, accepted it and went straight into COBOL programming.

'I am a wife first, a computer programmer afterwards,' Julia says and although that means not going on site and ending up with jobs that are less interesting, Julia has made that choice. She says, 'I don't necessarily get the best jobs to keep in project leading or to further my career, but that's a choice I have made, really.' She continues saying that when there are jobs going on site her manager continues to offer them, but accepts when 'he is beaten.' And she says 'I think it is a terrible shame that a lot of people are brainwashed into thinking they have got to go out to work in order to be anybody.'

A five-year projection sees Julia bringing up children, perhaps doing home-programming if she were bored or in need of money, but she has other interests and thinks she would not have to work to get an interest outside the kids. And in twenty years time? 'I might like to have a hand at something different — but yes, if I thought I could catch up with all the new technology. You spend a year doing something on 1900 and they invent a 2900 and you don't know a thing about it. It depends what the world is like in twenty years,' says Julia.

The sex-discrimination issue is a bit overdone according to Julia. 'I think if women fight as hard as men, they will get on as well.' She finds references like 'the girls over there' annoying, but thinks it has no actual effect on advancement (although she can speak only of her Dataskil experience).

'A woman tends to take criticism of her work more personally. So if somebody criticises a bloke's program he takes it as a criticism of his program. A woman takes it as a personal criticism and therefore might feel discriminated against.'

Julia thinks society has taken a positive attitude towards the single woman who must work to support herself, but a negative view of a married woman who considers marriage and family important enough to devote all her time to.

'I think it is a tremendous privilege and a tremendous responsibility ....I mean I have worked six years and I am quite happy doing that. I hope I shan't feel a cabbage sitting at home for a few years.'

SHARON

'I am not saying that there is a positive discrimination – that you won't get a job because you are a woman – but what I am saying is that all other things being equal between you and a male applicant, they (male interviewers) will consider you have an extra impediment over the male (applicant) if they know you are married.'

These are the words of Sharon, a 35-year-old principal consultant who just applied for a line management position and did not get it.

'I don't know of any women line managers, managers who can actually be said to be in computing in Dataskil,' says Sharon, noting there are women managers on the administrative and personnel side.

She describes the interview panel of three men as a 'self-selecting oligarchy.' In her experience, the technical part of the interview was 'very straightforward; very good; very non-discriminatory.' But personal details were attended to with such questions as 'if you got this job wouldn't your husband be ever so upset if his tea is not on the table when he gets home because you can't always guarantee your time of coming home?'

Sharon doubts that male applicants are faced with questions about their domestic arrangements, and believes this sort of questioning directed to a female employee could constitute a case which could be brought under the discrimination regulations.

Of bringing suit she says 'I wouldn't think it is worth doing because these poor innocents who form the committee believe probably that by interviewing a woman they have shown they don't discriminate. I believe they can't help what they do.' The fact that they cannot help what they do is a function of the age and background of the individuals who form today's company decision-making hierarchy, according to Sharon.

And she says just because Dataskil is in a high technology area does not mean it is more likely to have less discrimination as long as the decision-makers remain the same. Sharon sums up: 'perhaps that's a blow to the organisational image. I hope so.'

Sharon's parents left school at twelve and fourteen, her mother serving an apprenticeship as a tailoress and her father a skilled tool-maker. Sharon attended school in the East End of London and left grammar school with 'O' levels. She says the school was 'very, very anti-working class... and was clearly divided into those who came from the council estates and those who didn't.' She married at seventeen and went to live in Scotland. Her husband was middle-class, educated, and from a very political background, and they moved in a political circle which included socialist MPs and the like. As her background was extremely trade unionist and socialist, Sharon says, 'I found, strangely enough, that even at that age I could contribute to the conversation and hold my own with his people and realised that I would never achieve anything unless I got some formal qualifications – simply because a piece of paper makes it so much easier – it is the entrance ticket.'

Sharon did so well in her first year ONC mathematics course that she left and went to university to specialise in statistics – for which she had a great interest and aptitude. At university in Scotland, Sharon was able to participate in a counsellor scheme. The woman to whom she reported was available when Sharon required her, was very well known in the field of micro-analysis, 'and having made it herself, I suppose she had some interest in seeing other females doing the course,' says Sharon.

Towards the end of her university years there was a teacher shortage in Scotland, and Sharon conducted a battle with the careers advisor who was handing-out, preferentially to women, literature on teacher qualifications. 'I did have some argument with the careers officer that he shouldn't be doing this – you'll note it was a 'he' – because the line he was pushing was the usual 'this will fit in with your home and raising a family' which I resented – very much.'

Sharon says that no woman influenced her life positively. Rather she was negatively influenced and reacted against it. ('Seeing the way my mother was exploited during her lifetime.') Her mother 'for all those years of work' left £1500 and a £60 fur coat – the largest luxury investment she ever made. Sharon says she'll keep that coat and continue to wear it (although she doesn't like the idea of animals being cut up) because 'for someone who worked all her life in a trade that continues to exploit women at ridiculous rates of pay, it is a reminder to me not to let myself be put in that position – ever.' Sharon feels her mother died younger than she would have done because of the amount of work she did in her lifetime – both in and out of the home.

Sharon sees herself income-producing until retirement (or sudden wealth). She hopes to get into line-management within the year. And if she doesn't? 'I can either get very bitter and twisted or I can... continue on the technical side. I will make efforts to move into a line-management job. I can't think at the moment about not achieving because if I am going to achieve it, I have got to concentrate on doing so...'

And what about factors over which she has no control, such as sex discrimination in recruiting? Sharon says 'You can't blame not getting a job on discrimination – that's too simple and would stop you having a good look at yourself .... It would stop you being sufficiently self-critical to make any progress at all.' Sharon thinks that women in policy-making decisions are older than their equivalent male counterparts and that this situation is probably the effect of discrimination – a slowing rather than a stopping effect.

Some people say that women suffer discrimination due to their own self-defeating behaviour. Does Sharon agree?

'Yes I do. Women are just as much the product of conditioning in childhood as men, so I think you will quite often get a talented woman who has come from a background which says she should be at home looking after her family, and she will waver between the two. Every time she experiences success within her job, it will reinforce her in that direction, and she will begin moving up and forwards. But a very small challenge from someone close to her as to the 'rightness' of what she is doing, will bring her ego crashing down immediately and she will think 'Oh well I can do this, but I really should be looking after the children', which is very sad. It is guilt that results, I think, from the original conditioning that she should be fulfilling this function first. In fact, it is remarkable (the results of this) because over half of her mental effort will probably be in containing the guilt and maintaining the home, and the little mental energy that's left will probably do a good job. But not good enough. And not enough determination to move up. To compete higher.'

SUSAN

Susan is a 23-year-old senior programmer and comes from a working-class background in the North-East of England. She has a working mother – she is a secretary – and although her father is a public servant, in a job implying no need for numerical aptitude, Susan says he is very good with numbers. The other offspring, also female, is a maths teacher. Susan went to university, taking a business degree comprising maths, economics and computer science. 'I think it runs in the family,' says Susan, referring to the maths ability.

Of her schooling, Susan notes 'I went to grammar school which turned comprehensive after 2 years so I went to a different school. I was doing 'O' levels and got pushed into doing all arts subjects even though I was good at maths. I didn't want to do arts, so in the end I did double maths and geography. I hated geography, which makes me think if I'd been a boy they might have pushed me at 'O' level to maths, chemistry and physics.'

Susan, who joined Dataskil two years ago as a graduate trainee sees her career taking her into consultancy because the other obvious goal is management – 'I'm not the type of person to manage people really,' she says, adding that a manager is a bossy person who makes quick decisions.

There are not many female line-managers at Dataskil. 'I don't know why, really,' states Susan, 'Perhaps it's policy, but not many girls go into computing and I think it probably starts from school. Girls with mathematical backgrounds are not really encouraged.'

Susan says she suffers no sex discrimination at work, but feels pressure from people she knows in the North East – which is where she considers home. 'Where I come from people think there is something wrong with you if you are not married by, say, the age of twenty. That really annoys me – they think you shouldn't have a career.'

One of only three girls in a class of twenty-five at university, Susan says a university degree has given her no advantages at all, but does not regret it. Her early education is another matter. 'If I had been a boy I think they would have taken greater consideration about my choice of 'O' levels,' she concludes.

JANE

A 32-year-old database consultant, Jane is in her second period of employment with Dataskil, having once left because she did not like being 'body-shopped,' ie being on site for extended periods. Of that period she says, 'whether I didn't like it because I'm female or whether I don't like it because I'm married, or whether people just don't like it — I don't like being on site for a long period of time.'

Jane's siblings — she is the eldest of three — work in the building trade and in a factory. Her mother did not work outside the home and although her father was a trained electrician, he chose to work as a salesman, embarking upon various enterprises with which his wife assisted him.

Jane says she has a 'big beef' about her secondary modern school education: there were no sciences 'other than the occasional exploding or floating can,' and no languages. She was virtually pushed towards all arts 'O' levels but seems grateful she was 'allowed' 'O' levels and didn't have to leave after the 4th year to do the only job possible — work at Woolies. Jane remembers that out of thirty people in the 5th form, three went on to further education. 'I know there were people there that left when they were 16 and that were better than me at something — I mean, they're just bank clerks.'

High school was an experience Jane says she 'goofed up.' She enrolled in what she says were inappropriate classes. 'I don't know ... perhaps I didn't read enough and I didn't ask the right questions ...but it did just seem that you were channelled.' So teachers training college it was to be. 'Well, I did (apply for) a couple, but I wasn't really interested and my old school maths teacher had sort of got computing in my mind, and my father knew this guy in computing and I had a chat with him, so I decided I wanted to do computing. I saw an ad. I think it was in the Telegraph for North Staff Polytechnic, for an HND in computing. You see with only 2 'A' levels you don't think about a degree. I mean your mind's channelled down. I think I could have done it standing on my head actually. So I got an HND in maths, stats and computing.'

Jane began computing at a British Transport facility and after four years left when she felt she was being pushed to take a promotion she did not want. She then joined Dataskil, left after 2½ years to work for a government body which was piloting 'not a bad bit' of Dataskil software. She then returned three years ago to Dataskil to work on the team that developed that software.

The people Jane works with are men and she says there are incidents .... 'I can go up to a Xerox room and if a bloke walks in and if I am the only woman in there, very often he will ask me to do his xeroxing for him... that annoys me intensely. But they don't know you, you see.'

Jane goes on to say that if there is a gift to be collected for her manager, he will suggest she do it. 'There is that sort of assumption. But that same manager has given me pay rises without my asking for them,' she notes.

Jane thinks there are 'occasional characters' who take a bit longer to be convinced that she knows what she is talking about. She thinks women have to try harder than men to prove themselves — usually to men. 'But I don't know,' she says, 'I'd have to dress in drag and go and see customers as the same person to see what the reaction is.'

The obvious lack of females in line-management positions is a situation Jane has observed. She herself says being a manager would be 'sheer hell. I would rather advance on the technical side.'

About sex prejudices, Jane says she wishes the Xerox incidents didn't ever happen, but feels no effects from them. 'I think possibly computing is one of the better industries because it's a modern one,' she concludes.

Appendix 2
Bibliography

CHAPTER 1

Arratoon A, Confused Careers Advice (review), *Computing*, 20/11/80

Carlyle D, *Careers in Computing*, Kogan Page, 1980

Cooley M, The Place of Daphne in the World of Apollo, *Computing*, 9/10/80

Davies D, The Stormy Life of the World's First Programmer, *Computer Weekly*, 10/1/80

Dooley A, 'Association for Women in Computing' Formed, *Computerworld*, 18/12/78, p 5

Hunt J and Adams S, *Women, Work and Trade Union Organisation*, WEA, 9 Upper Berkeley Street, London W1H 8BX

Kirchner J, WIP Establishing 'Old Girl Network', *Computerworld*, 22/9/80, p 24

Moore D L, *Ada, Countess of Lovelace*, John Murray, London, 1977

Minimum Wages for Women, An Examination of Women's Earnings in Industries Covered by Wages Councils, A Low Pay Unit research project funded by the Equal Opportunities Commission, September 1980

Smedley J, A Sex by themselves, *Data Systems*, June 1970, pp 26-29, 46

Smith W D, Pioneer in Computers, *New York Times*, 5/9/71

Turner F, Programme that has Women Turned On..., *Watford Echo*, 16/1/76

Two Million Women are Underpaid, Says Report, *Guardian*, 23/10/80

Werneke D, The Economic Slowdown and Women's Employment Opportunities, *International Labour Review*, Vol 117, No 1, January-February 1978

Winkler C, AWC Chief Urges Women to Know Hardware, *Computerworld*, 9/6/80, p 18

Winkler C, 'Old Girl Networks' Help Women to Get Ahead', *Computerworld*, 6/10/80, p 22

Women are Left Behind in Equal Rights Struggle, *Computing*, 16/10/80, p 11

Women Have Nearly Made It, *Computer Weekly*, 23/10/80

Zalud B, Dr Ruth M Davies: DPMA Computer Sciences Man-of-the Year, *Data Management*, October 1979, pp 37-39

Zientara M, Women in DP Advised on Career Planning, *Computerworld*, 9/6/80, p 20

CHAPTER 2

A Real Place for Women in Engineering, *Industrial and Commercial Training*, December 1979

Arnst C, Sexism in DP Industry a Controversial Issue in '75, *Computerworld*, 31/12/75 - 5/1/76, p 13

Barton C et al, Technically Qualified Manpower: Are Women Filling the Gap? *Personnel Management*, May 1980, pp 44-47

Berg K, *Women's Position in the Data Processing Professions*, International Congress of Data Processing, Berlin, October 1980

Biryukova A P, Special Protective Legislation and Equality of Opportunity for Women Workers in the USSR, *International Labour Review*, January/February 1980, pp 51-65

Connell H B, Special Protective Legislation of Equality of Employment Opportunity for Women in Australia, *International Labour Review*, March/April 1980, pp 199-216

Dasey R and Lamb J, Pin Ups or Pin Money: the Same Old Picture, *Computing*, 2/10/80

Dhanens T P, Implications of the new EEOC Guidelines, *Personnel*, September/October 1979, pp 32-39

Dix C, The Issue of the ERA, *Guardian*, 21/10/80

Dunne N, Equal Rights Fail to Move the Majority, *Financial Times*, 15/10/77

Dwyer P, Humpty Dumpty Challenge for Women Over Jobs, Pay and Training Opportunities, *Electronics Times*, 14/2/80, pp 28-29

Gilchrist B and Kapur R, *Computer Industry Employment*, AFIPS Press, Montvale N J, 1974

Glucklich P and Povall M, Equal Opportunities: A Case for Action in Default of the Law, *Personnel Management*, January 1979, pp 28-31

Gomori E, Special Protective Legislation and Equality of Employment Opportunity for Women in Hungary, *International Labour Review*, January/February 1980, pp 67-77

Grossman R, Silicon's Ugly Secret: the Asian Assembly Lines, *Computing*, 6/9/79, pp 18-20

Harold S, *The Role of Women in Computing*, F International, 1973, pp 195-215

Hunt A, *OPCS: Survey of Management Attitudes and Practices Towards Women at Work*, HMSO, 1975

Hutt C, *Males and Females*, Penguin, 1972

Kraft P and Biggar L, Women Suffer on Bottom of DP Line, *Computing*, 19/7/79, pp 14-15

Lamb J and Dasey R, Pin Ups or Pin Money: the Same Old Picture, *Computing*, 2/10/80

Legislating for Equality, *European Industrial Relations Review*, March 1979, pp 6-7

London School of Economics review of the Implementation of the Equal Pay and Sex Discrimination Acts for three years, for 1974-1977, in 26 organisations.

Mamrak S A and Montanelli R G, Computer Science Faculties: The Current Status of Minorities and Women, *Communications of the ACM*, February 1978, pp 115-119

Massey A, Beyond the Prejudice It Can be a Good Life, *Engineer*, 10/4/80, pp 34-36

McNurlin B C, EEO Commitment Can Erase DP's Anti-Women Bias, *Computerworld*, 27/9/76, p 28

Men and Women, Key Figures, Swedish Committee for Equality at Work, Stockholm, 1979

Montanelli R G and Mamrak S A, The Status of Women and Minorities in Academic Computer Science, *Communications of the ACM*, October 1976, pp 578-581

Murray M, Never Mind Equality – Feel the Quantity, *Education and Training*, November/December 1980, pp 313-314, 317

National Science Foundation, *Women and Minorities in Science and Engineering*, NSF, 77-304, 1977

National Science Foundation, *US Scientists and Engineers, 1974*, NSF, 76-329, 1976

New Equal Opportunities Legislation for Ireland, *European Industrial Relations Review*, July 1977, pp 6-9

Nickell S J, Trade Unions and the Position of Women in the Industrial Wage Structure, *British Journal of Industrial Relations*, July 1977

Nielson R, Special Protective Legislation for Women in the Nordic Countries, *International Labour Review*, January/February 1980, pp 39-49

Peterson L L, *The Status of Women in Health Science Computing*, National Computer Conference, 1979

Poe P, Why Don't More Women Get into DP? *Computer Weekly*, 30/10/80

Project Opens Computer Science Jobs to Women, *Computerworld*, 28/7/80, p 17

Protective Laws in Need of Reform, *European Industrial Relations Review*, April 1980, pp 9-10

Ramaley J A (ed), *Covert Discrimination and Women in the Sciences*, Westview Press for American Association for the Advancement of Science, AAAS Selected Symposium 14, 1978

Rose C and Bolus S M, Women in the Computer Sciences, *Computer*, August 1980, p 79

Rosenberg M, Lack of Women DPers Seen 'Severe Loss', *Computerworld*, 20/11/78

Schein V E, Sex Role Stereotyping, Ability and Performance: Prior Research and New Directions, *Personnel Psychology*, Summer 1978, pp 259-268

Shirley S, *Women in Data Processing*, International Congress of Data Processing, Berlin, 1980

Should Women Work Night Shifts? *The Times*, 25/10/77, p 16

Simpson D, Time to Woo Back the Women, *Data Processing*, September 1979, pp 12, 14

Stone J, Survey Reveals Discrimination at 36% of DP Centres, *Computerworld*, 7 March 1977, p 15

Technical, Personal Seminars Geared to Women, *Computerworld*, 15/9/80, p 28

Turner F, She Has Got Computing Video-Taped, *Aberdeen Press*, 7/1/76

Wainwright D, *Discrimination in Employment*, Associated Business Press, London, 1979

Walsh D, The Memoirs of a Progra-MS, *Computer Weekly*, 14/7/77, pp 16-17

Weber R E and Gilchrist B, Discrimination in the Employment of Women in the Computer Industry, *Communications of the ACM*, July 1975, pp 416-418

Women in Industry, The Industrial Society, October 1980

Women in Traditionally Male Jobs: The Experiences of Ten Public Utility Companies, US Department of Labour, R & D Monograph 65, 1978

Wood H M, *Women and Minorities in the Computer Professions*, National Computer Conference, 1979

Woodruff C K, Data Processing People — Are They Really Different? *Information and Management*, October 1980, pp 133-139

CHAPTER 3

Anderson E, Why Aren't There More Women in the Boardroom? *Director*, November 1979, pp 62-63

Bass B M, *PROFAIR: A Program About Working With Women*, Transnational Programs Corporation, 1971

Bringing Women into Computer Management, *EDP Analyzer*, August 1976, pp 1-14

Crisp J, Why Can't a Woman Be More Like a Manager?, *Financial Times*, 1/8/78

Dasey R and Lamb J, Pin Ups or Pin Money: the Same Old Picture, *Computing*, 2/10/80, pp 16-17

Davidson M and Cooper C, The Extra Pressures on Women Executives, *Personnel Management*, June 1980, pp 48-51

Davidson M and Cooper C, The Women Under Pressure, *Guardian*, 9/10/80, p 20

Davidson M and Cooper C, What Women Managers Face, *Management Today*, February 1981, pp 80-83

Delamaide D, Why German Women Are Kept Out of the Executive World, *Financial Times*, 4/9/79

Dooley A, Women DP'ers Cite Promotion Bias, *Computerworld*, 5/3/79

Dooley A, Profile of a Woman DPer in Management, *Computerworld*, 5/3/79

Harvey C, How Women Compete in the Computer Industry, *Computer Weekly*, 8/6/78

Hennig M and Jardim A, *The Managerial Woman*, Pan 1979

Hunt A, *OPCS: Survey of Management Attitudes and Practices Towards Women at Work*, HMSO, 1975

Kanter R M, *Men and Women of the Corporation*, Basic Books, NY, 1977

Koehn H E, Attitude: the Success Element for Women in Business, *Journal of Systems Management*, March 1976, pp 12-15

Koff I A and Handlon J H, Women in Management: Keys to Success or Failure, *The Personnel Administrator*, American Society for Personnel Administration, April 1975

Lamb J and Dasey R, Pin Ups or Pin Money: the Same Old Picture, *Computing*, 2/10/80

Levitin T et al, Sex Discrimination Against the American Working Woman, *Women in the Professions*, Sage Publications, 1971

McRae H, Why British Women Deserve a Seat on the Board, *Guardian*, 8/8/80

Mirides E and Cote A, Women in Management: Strategies for Removing the Barriers, *The Personnel Administrator*, April 1980, pp 25-28, 48

Reif W E et al, Exploding Some Myths About Women Managers, *California Management Review*, Summer 1975, pp 72-79

Richbell S, De Facto Discrimination and How to Kick the Habit, *Personnel Management*, November 1976

Robertson W, How Harvard Women MBAs Are Doing, *Economic Impact*, Number 2, 1979, pp 52-55

Sanders A T, Why More Women Should be DP Managers, *Canadian Datasystems*, June 1978, pp 49-51

Schroeder E, Women Win a Surprise Victory in Operation Executive, *Financial Times*, 21/10/80

Sex Discrimination in Management and Computing, *Data Processing*, December 1977/January 1978, pp 18-23

Siegel G, The Best Man for the Job May Be a Woman, *Datamation*, June 1976, pp 196-200

Snyders J and Miles M, Women in Management, *Computer Decisions*, August 1980, pp 90-97

The Business Woman, *Data Processing*, December 1980/January 1980, pp 12-13

The Feminist Manager, *Management Today*, April 1979, pp 90-92, 96-97, 150, 152

Wainwright D, *Discrimination in Employment*, Associated Business Press, 1979

Walsh D, The Memoirs of a Progra-MS, *Computer Weekly*, 14/7/77, pp 16-17

Webster G and Spooner P, Women in Management, *Chief Executive*, December 1980

Wix B, *Effective Management by Including Women in Management Tasks*, International Congress of Data Processing, Berlin, October 1980

Women in Industry, The Industrial Society, October 1980

Women in Management: A Conversation, *Datamation*, April 1980, pp 131-132, 134, 136, 139-140

Women in Traditionally Male Jobs: The Experiences of Ten Public Utility Companies, R & D Monograph 65, US Department of Labour

CHAPTER 4

Apex View of Office Technology, *International Word Processing Report*, Volume 4/12, 1st April 1979

Asha P, *Problems of the Introduction of EDP Systems in Regard to Female Personnel in Industrial as well as in Developing Countries*, International Congress of Data Processing, Berlin, October 1980

Automating the Office, CIS Report, *The New Technology*

Barron I and Curnow R, *The Future With Microelectronics*, Frances Pinter, London, 1979

Bird E, *Information Technology in the Office: the Impact on Women's Jobs*, A Research Project Funded by the Equal Opportunities Commission, September 1980

Birnbaum R, *Health Hazards of Visual Display Units*, Information and Advisory Service, London School of Hygiene and Tropical Medicine, March 1978

Black H, Radiation Scare May Become Industrial Relations Issue, *Canadian Data Systems*, December 1980, pp 64-65

British Optical Information Council, Opticians' Advice on VDU Operator Eye Problems, *Modern Office and Data Management*, August 1980, pp 22-24

Busch G, Ergonomic Problems with VDUs in the Banking and Insurance Industries, *Report for FIET USA*, 1976, pp 17-18

Cakir A et al, *The VDT Manual*, IFRA, Germany, 1979

Church L, Report Fuels Work and Women Debate, *Computing*, 23/10/80, p 8

Collins S, Women and Chips, *Spare Rib*, No. 83, June 1979, pp 19-22

Damodaran L et al, *Designing Systems for People*, NCC Publications, 1980

Guide to Health Hazards of Visual Display Units, An ASTMS Policy Document, Association of Scientific, Technical and Managerial Staffs

Jenkins C and Sherman B, *The Collapse of Work*, Eyre Methuen, London, 1979

Krass P, How the WP Revolution Affects US Office Workers, *Computer Weekly*, 2/10/80

McMahon F, Office Drudges and the Bosses Who Can't Spell, *Computing*, 6/3/80, pp 18-19

New Deal for Office Staff, AUEW TASS

Nora-S and Minc A, *L'information de la societe*, Documentation Francaise, Paris, May 1978

Office Technology, The Trade Union Response, Association of Professional Executive, Clerical and Computer Staff

Parks T H, How to be Run Off One's Feet in a More Up-to-Date Electronic Fashion, *Guardian*, 19/11/80

Pearce B, Starting in the Face of a Big Small Screen Scare, *Computing*, 17/4/80, pp 20-21

Pentney J, Terminal Health, *Computer Age*, January 1981, pp 91-92

Price S G, *Introducing the Electronic Office*, NCC Publications, 1979

Siemens, *Internal Report on Impact of Office Technology*, Germany, 1978. (Discussed by David Dangelmayer, The Job Killers of Germany, *New Scientist*, 8/6/78, p 650)

Simons G L, *The Uses of Microprocessors*, NCC Publications, 1980

Sleigh J et al, *The Manpower Implications of Microelectronic Technology*, Department of Employment, HMSO, London, 1979

The Office Revolution, *Data Processing*, May 1978, pp 27-30, 32, 34

Virgo P, *Cashing in on the Chips*, Conservative Political Centre, London, May 1979

Warr A, Programmed for Misery, *Guardian*, 4/9/80

CHAPTER 5

Calm View of Management, *Datamation*, August 1976, pp 13-14

Clutterbuck D (i), This Typist is Paid to Stay at Home, *International Management*, October 1979, pp 49-50

Clutterbuck D (ii), New Deal for Part-Time Workers, *International Management*, October 1979, pp 40-41, 44, 47

Dooley A, Service Bureau's Women DPers Work at Home, *Computerworld*, 28/5/79, pp 11-12

Filling Jobs from Untapped Sources, *Computer Weekly*, 28/8/80, p 6

Finding Qualified EDP Personnel, *EDP Analyzer*, August 1980, pp 1-12

F is for Fascinating, *Oxfordshire Businessman*, June 1980

Going Freelance, talk delivered to BCS, March 1980, F International

Morris J, *Computer Weekly*, 8/11/79, p 6

Morris J, Satisfying 'Home' Career — and Hours are Flexible, *Computer Weekly*, 15/11/79, p 6

Myers E, Home is Where the Work Is, *Datamation*, February 1980, pp 77-79

Shaw A, A Programme for Ideal Living, *Computer Weekly*, 11/9/80

Shirley S, Ill Met By Moonlight, *Computer Weekly*, 11/9/80

The Career Woman's Family Business, *Computer Talk*, 14/3/79

Walsh W, Angela Has the Key to Careers at Home, *Manchester Evening News*, 15/5/79

When Women Stay Home to Go Out to Work, *Industrial and Business News*, August 1980

Woollcombe J, Computers Need People, *The Times*, 20/10/70, p 19

Appendix 3

Plates

1 Countess Ada Lovelace, world's first programmer

2 Captain Grace Hopper, Cobol pioneer

3 Mrs Pam Morton, Senior Lecturer in Systems Analysis in Thames Polytechnic's television studios, training Computing Science students in systems investigation techniques

4 Miss P M Woodman, Managing Director, Pamela Woodman Associates

5 Mrs Steve Shirley, OBE, founder of F International

6 F International panel members working on site

7 Home-based Project Manager (F International)

8 Home-based Programmer (F International) using terminal

9 F International panel members working on site

10 Mrs Joy Whitehead (South Eastern Electricity Board) using interactive terminal to answer telephone enquiries

11 Typical product advertisement: named product, unnamed woman

1 Countess Ada Lovelace, world's first programmer

2 Captain Grace Hopper, Cobol pioneer

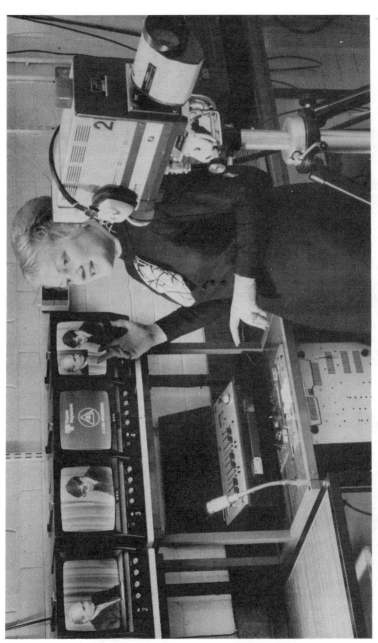

3 Mrs Pam Morton, Senior Lecturer in Systems Analysis in Thames Polytechnic's television studios, training Computing Science students in systems investigation techniques

4   Miss P M Woodman, Managing Director,
Pamela Woodman Associates

5 Mrs Steve Shirley, OBE, founder of F International

6 F International panel members working on site

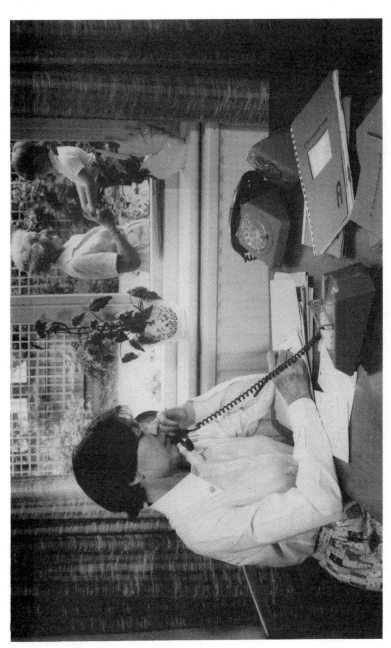

7   Home-based Project Manager (F International)

8 Home-based Programmer (F International) using terminal

9 F International panel members working on site

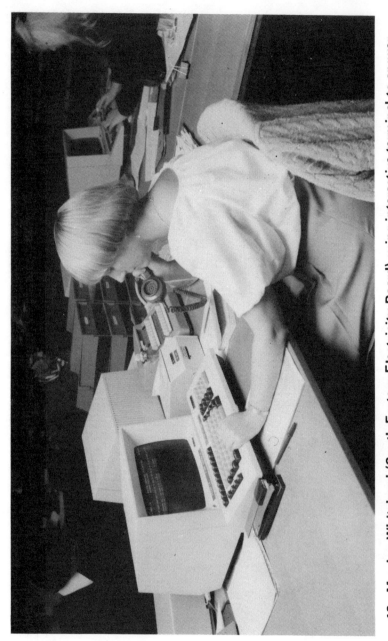

10 Mrs Joy Whitehead (South Eastern Electricity Board) using interactive terminal to answer telephone enquiries

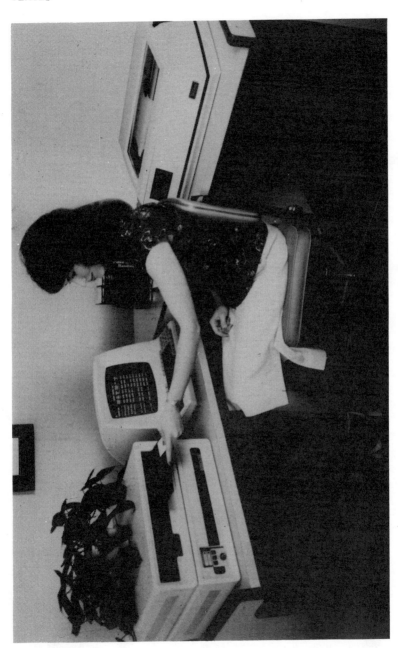

11 Typical product advertisement: named product, unnamed woman

Appendix 4

Index
(Subjects and Names)

SUBJECTS

ACM (Association for Computing
  Machinery) 21
ADA 27
Advertisements 24, 32-35, 46, 54, 165
Advertising Standards Authority (ASA) 33, 35
AERE 137, 139
Analytical Engine 26-27
ANSI X3.4 Committee 28
Anti-discrimination programmes 47-48, 51
APEX 65-66, 114, 116, 117,
  118, 121, 127-128

Apprenticeships 74
Aptitudes 77, 95-96
Area Wage Surveys (US) 60
ASA (Advertising Standards Authority) 33, 35
Asian women 7, 56-58
ASK Computer Services 100
Assembly work 56
Association for Computing
  Machinery (ACM) 21
Association for Women in Computing
  (AWC) 21, 22, 23, 24, 25, 92
Association for Women in Science
  (AWIS) 21, 23
ASTMS 20, 37, 118, 128
Australia 45
Automobile Association 115, 137
AWC (Association for Women in
  Computing) 21, 22, 23, 24, 25, 92
AWIS (Association for Women in
  Science) 21, 22, 23
AWIS Educational Foundation 21

Banking, Insurance and Finance
  Union (Bifu) 121
Barclays Bank International 105
Barts Hospital, London 31
Bernoulli numbers 27
British Computer Society (BCS) 29

British Gas	137
British Institute of Management	83, 105, 139
British International Paper Ltd	31
British Optical Information Council (BOIC)	126
Bureau of Ordnance Computation Project (Harvard)	28
Business Woman of the Year Award	29
California	57, 58
Camco 825MP guillotine	110
Camden Borough Council	105
Canada	126
Canon NP80 copier	110
Carnegie Mellon University	31
Careers in Computing	35
Cartoons	35
Case studies	155-166
CBI	104
CBI Award for Employee Involvement	85
CEGB	119
Characteristics of women	93-98
Chemical Analysis of Women	35
Chemical Engineering	32
Chemicals, toxic	58
Civil Rights Act (US)	61, 64
Civil Service Building Society	101-102
COBOL	28, 159
CODASYL	28
Commercial Union Assurance Group (CU)	142
Computer Management Group (Scotland)	85
Computer Services Association (CSA)	132
Computers, Systems and Electronics Requirements Board (CSERB)	29
Computerwoche	66-67
Computerworld	61
Congress (US)	21
Consciousness raising	26, 80, 92, 155

Contract Programming Services (ICL)	145
Control Data Institut (Frankfurt)	94
Cosmopolitan	54
Court of Appeal	47
CPSA	118, 127
Culham Laboratory	55
Data entry	19
Datamation	61
Data Processing Management Association	28, 31, 93
Data processing managers (See also Managers)	19, 30, 56, 66-67, 99-104, 107-108
Dataskil	67-68, 153, 155-166
Department of Agriculture (US)	107
Department of Education and Science (UK)	73
Department of Employment (US)	98
Department of Industry (UK)	70
Deskilling	110, 111, 112, 118-123
Department of Labour (US)	50, 59, 89
Difference Engine	26
Discrimination	18-19, 21, 37, 38, 41, 43, 47, 54, 55, 59-71, 72, 75-76, 85-88, 89-90, 98-99, 100, 103-104, 153, 155, 160, 161, 162-163, 164, 165
Displaywriter	120
DPMA 'Man of the Year' Award	28, 30-31
Eastern Europe	85
EAT (Employment Appeal Tribunal)	47
Eckert-Mauchley Computer Corporation	28

Education   20, 31, 35, 51, 61, 72-
                                             81, 84, 85, 106, 150-
                                             151, 155, 159, 162,
                                             164, 165
EEC (European Economic Community)   44-45
Employment   — in data processing   25, 37-38, 41, 59-71,
                                             112-118, 119
             — in general   15-16, 45-54, 70, 112
   (See also Job Security)
Employment Appeal Tribunal (EAT)   47
Employment Protection Act   46
Engineering Industry Training Board
   (EITB)   75-76
English Electric   142
Eniac   62-63, 155
'Eniac girls'   62-63
Equal Opportunities Commission (EOC)   18, 33, 44, 46, 104,
                                             151
Equal opportunities policies   47-48, 51-54, 75-76,
                                             80, 90-93, 104-107,
                                             108, 150-151
Equal Pay Act (UK)   16, 18, 43-44, 45-46,
                                             48, 55, 65
Equal Pay Act (US)   61
Equal Rights Amendment (ERA)   45
ERA (Equal Rights Amendment)   45
Ergonomics   126-127, 128
European Economic Community (EEC)   44-45
Eyesight   58, 123-128

F2   137
Fairchild   57
Ferranti   144
Finland   84
Finniston Committee   74
F International Ltd   29, 55, 70, 132-133,
                                             136-140, 141, 142,
                                             151
France   54, 125, 135

Freelance Programmers Ltd   29, 30, 132-133, 142
Freelance work   131-147

'Gamesmanship'   22, 23
GEC-Elliott Computer Software
    Company   133
GEC Measurement Ltd   134
General Electric   100
Girls and Science   73

Hackney Borough Council   105
Halifax Building Society   113
Health   7, 57-58, 123-128
Heidrick & Struggles   92
Heights Inc   141-142
Holland   135
Home-based work   131-147
Honeywell   71,. 135
House of Representatives (US)   45
Hungary   45

IBM   42, 65, 120
ICI   104-105
ICL   29, 102, 137, 144,
                                             145-146
ICL Contract Programming   145-146
ILEA   74
Indonesia   57
Industrial Tribunal   46
Institute of Bankers   84, 88
Institute of Chartered Accountants   84
Institute of Data Processing   104, 139
Institute of Directors   83
Institute of Supervisory Management   84
Institution of Civil Engineers   84
Institution of Mechanical Engineers   83
Intel   56, 57
International Congress of Data
    Processing (Berlin, 1980)   19, 65, 94
Ireland   45

Italy   54, 84

Job security   18, 110, 111-118, 119,
                                                  120, 134-135
Johnson O'Connor Research Foundation   95
Journals   32-34
J Sainsbury Ltd   105

Kent Industrial Measurements   76
Key Communications   67
Key-punch operators   19
Kienbaum Consultants   66-67, 88

Law Society   84
Legislation   16, 18, 30, 43-47, 57,
                                                  80-81, 150
LeHigh University   42
Leyland International   139
Liebrecht Personnel Consultants   88
Lister Hill National Centre for
    Biomedical Communication   31
Liverpool Stock Exchange   36
Lloyds Bank   137
Logica   113
London School of Economics (LSE)
    research project   46-47
London Science Museum   31
Low Pay Unit   18
LSE research project   46-47
Lucas Industries   134

Macon (Gaul)   8
Malaysia   56
Management   19, 30, 31, 53, 54, 84,
                                                  86, 97, 105, 113
Management and Executive Selection   70

Managers
  (See also Data processing managers)   57, 86, 88-89, 92-93,
                                          97, 98, 101, 106, 107,
                                          113
Manhattan Project   63
Manpower Services Commission (MSC)   105
Manufacturing   7, 18, 19, 56-58, 70,
                                          72

Media images   19, 32-37
Microprocessors   110
Micro Switch   135-136
Miniature relays   33
Moore School of Electrical Engineering   62-63
Motorola Communications Group   35
Multiplexer   33
'Myths'   34, 89, 93, 95, 96

NALGO   110, 127
National Bureau of Standards (NBS)   31, 64
National Coal Board   113
National Computer Conference (NCC)   42, 64, 68
National Computing Centre (NCC)   68-69, 70-71, 76-77,
                                         110

National Science Foundation (US)   64-65, 78, 80
Natural wastage   114, 116
NCR   142
NEDO report   21
Netherlands   45, 84
'Networking'   22, 23-24, 25, 72, 80,
                                        154

Networking   23
New York State University   120
New York Times   24
Norway   54, 67, 84, 126, 134
Norwegian Computer Society   67
NUJ   127

Office automation   109-129
Oglaend, Jonas   134
Open University   137

ORDVAC computer — 31

Pamela Woodman Associates (PWA) — 142-144
Parity — 22
Part-time work — 68, 131-147
Pay — in data processing — 53, 57, 59-61, 65-67, 78
— in general — 16-18
Penang — 56, 58
Perception of discrimination — 15, 85-86
Philippines — 57
Programmers — 28, 30, 55-56, 60, 62, 63, 64, 65, 68, 99, 131, 133-135, 140, 141, 143-144, 145-146, 159
Promotion — 53
Pronouns, use of — 35
Provident Financial Group — 113

Rank Xerox — 52-54
Rank Xerox 9400 copier — 110
Recession — 18, 38, 70, 111-112, 115, 118, 132, 150, 152
Recruitment — 48-49, 53, 75, 76, 78, 87, 91-92, 132-133, 163
Remington Rand Corporation — 28
Robert Sherry & Associates — 144-145
Robotics — 31

Scapegoating — 16, 62
SEAC computer — 31
Security of employment — 18
Service industries — 16, 18
Sex Discrimination Act (UK) — 43-44, 45-46, 48, 65, 104
Sexism — 15-16, 33-37, 41-42, 56

'Shakey' robot   31
Shift work   55, 57, 134
Siemens   114
Silicon chips   7
Silicon wafers   58
Silicon Valley   58
Singapore   57
Software Sciences Ltd   30
SOGAT   118
South-East Asia   56-58, 72
Southern California Edison (SCE)   91
Southern California University   85
South Korea   57
Sperry Univac   100
SRI International   31
Steps to take
   (See Equal opportunities policies)
Stereotypes   8, 15-16, 32, 35, 42-
                                        43, 72, 80, 87, 93, 97,
                                        99, 106, 107, 151
Stress   93, 98-100
Sweden   84, 135
Systems analysts   60

Taiwan   57
TASS   127
Technicians   24
Telecommunications   20, 24, 25
Texas University   80
Thailand   57
Thames Polytechnic   31, 76
Third World   7, 19, 151-152
Threshold Scheme   76-77
'Tokenism'   97, 105, 120, 128
TOPS   102
Trade unions
   (See also individual unions)   57-58, 123, 127-128
Treaty of Rome   44
TUC   109, 127

UCCA   76
UK   20, 25, 44, 45-46, 50,
                                              51, 65-66, 74-80, 83-
                                              85, 98, 104, 108, 112-
                                              113, 114-115, 116,
                                              132, 134

UK Atomic Weapons Research
    Establishment   55
UK Industrial Society   51
UNICOM   113
Unilever   137, 142
UNIVAC 1   31
US   20, 23, 25, 45, 50, 54,
                                              59, 60, 61, 62-64, 66,
                                              76, 78-80, 84, 85, 91,
                                              99, 100, 106, 108,
                                              112-113, 133, 136
US Department of Defense   31
US National Data Processing Service   30
US Navy   28, 31
USSR   45, 76, 85

Vector Graphic   100-101
Visual display units (VDUs)   123-128
Volkswagen (GB)   137

War Department (US)   62-63
Wells Fargo Bank   136
West Germany   20, 34, 54, 66-67, 88-
                                              89, 114, 135
WIP (Women in Information Processing)   22, 23
'Woman's Place'   8
'Women and Computing'   8
Women in Data-Processing   22, 24
Women in Information Processing   22, 23
Women in Management   105
Women in Science programme (NSF)   80
Word processing market   109-110, 116-117
Word processors   109, 110, 113-129

Yale University   28

NAMES

Adams, Elizabeth Shaw	92
Aiken, Howard	28
Allen, Jean	134
Aquinas, Thomas	8
Arratoon, Angela	35
Avent, Catherine	74
Babbage, Charles	26-27
Beckreck, Laurence	36
Berg, Kirsti	20, 67
Bird, Emma	111, 115-118, 121, 125
Broom, Janet	144
Brown, Robert	25
Buesst, Ursula	139
Busch, Dr G	124
Byron, Lord	26
Callies, Jean-Marie	125
Carlyle, D	35
Carney, Marion	102
Chapman, B	139
Charmer, Gillian	30
Cochran, Anita	21
Cooley, Mike	37
Cropper, Hilary	146
Crorie, Sue	140
Darwin, Charles	8
Dasey, Robyn	65
Davis, Ruth	31
Dorn, Philip	120
Durkin, J J	95-96
Else, Liz	8
Ely, Carole	101
Fox, Jean	139

Fuchs, Eckhard   19

Ginger, Angela   140

Hale, Louise   135
Harold, Suzette   55, 70, 138-139
Harp, Lore   101
Harvey, Christine   70
Hassman, Denise   24
Hecht, Charles P   54
Hendershot, T   107
Hennig, Margaret   93
Hopper, Grace Murray   27-29, 30-31, 184
Howells, J B   34
Hume, Fenella   76
Hunter, Joanna   34
Hutt, Corinne   73
Hypatia   27

James, Luanne   141
Jardim, Anne   93
Jones, Sonya Howell   71, 103

Kraft, Philip   120
Kurtzig, Sandra   100

Langley, Carole   36
Lardner, Dr   26
Law, Kay   71
Leitman, William J   25
Lennon, Janet   139
Lewis, Cherry   30
Lewis, Marion   31
Lightfoot, Judith   61
Lovelace, Ada   26-27, 183

Macdonald, Eleanor   105
Macdonald, Miriam   101-102
Martin, Margaret   144
Mason, Ida   42

Matteucci, Joanne   34
McCullough, Ruth   37
McDonald-Ross, Joyce   30
McLane, Helen   92
Menabrea, L F   27
Mendoza, Estelle   30
Miller, Janice   22
Morton, Pamela   31, 185

Nussbaum, Karen   120-121

Ogilvie, F   70

Payne, Elizabeth   104
Pena, Brenda   24
Poe, Pamela   67-68, 153
Pond, Chris   18
Price, Linda   47
Pugh, Jane   31

Roberts, Jan   31
Russell, Anne   141

Savings, Lynette   121
Scattergood, Marilyn   146
Sheilham, Teresa   140
Shirley, Steve (Stephanie)   29, 30,   31,   65,
                                      136-137, 138, 140,
                                      187
Smedley, Jill   29
Steel, Letitia   47
Stephenson, Miriam   30
Stott, Christine   71, 102-103

Taylor, Diane   139
Tutt, Penny   139

Urach, Christine, Fürstin von   20

Welch, Mary Scott   23

Whitehead, Joy	192
Wiersma, D T C	34
Wix, Barbara	94
Wood, Helen M	64
Wood, Marion	85
Woodman, Pamela	142-143, 144, 186